ENTHUSIAST'S RESTORATION MANUAL™

Classic Car Electrics

Tips, techniques & step-by-step repair, restoration & maintenance procedures

Other great books from Veloce –

Speedpro Series
4-Cylinder Engine Short Block High-Performance Manual – New Updated & Revised Edition (Hammill)
Alfa Romeo DOHC High-performance Manual (Kartalamakis)
Alfa Romeo V6 Engine High-performance Manual (Kartalamakis)
BMC 998cc A-series Engine, How to Power Tune (Hammill)
1275cc A-series High-performance Manual (Hammill)
Camshafts – How to Choose & Time Them For Maximum Power (Hammill)
Competition Car Datalogging Manual, The (Templeman)
Cylinder Heads, How to Build, Modify & Power Tune – Updated & Revised Edition (Burgess & Gollan)
Distributor-type Ignition Systems, How to Build & Power Tune – New 3rd Edition (Hammill)
Fast Road Car, How to Plan and Build – Revised & Updated Colour New Edition (Stapleton)
Ford SOHC 'Pinto' & Sierra Cosworth DOHC Engines, How to Power Tune – Updated & Enlarged Edition (Hammill)
Ford V8, How to Power Tune Small Block Engines (Hammill)
Harley-Davidson Evolution Engines, How to Build & Power Tune (Hammill)
Holley Carburetors, How to Build & Power Tune – Revised & Updated Edition (Hammill)
Honda Civic Type R High-Performance Manual, The (Cowland & Clifford)
Jaguar XK Engines, How to Power Tune – Revised & Updated Colour Edition (Hammill)
Land Rover Discovery, Defender & Range Rover – How to Modify Coil Sprung Models for High Performance & Off-Road Action (Hosier)
MG Midget & Austin-Healey Sprite, How to Power Tune – New 3rd Edition (Stapleton)
MGB 4-cylinder Engine, How to Power Tune (Burgess)
MGB V8 Power, How to Give Your – Third Colour Edition (Williams)
MGB, MGC & MGB V8, How to Improve – New 2nd Edition (Williams)
Mini Engines, How to Power Tune On a Small Budget – Colour Edition (Hammill)
Motorcycle-engined Racing Car, How to Build (Pashley)
Motorsport, Getting Started in (Collins)
Nissan GT-R High-performance Manual, The (Gorodji)
Nitrous Oxide High-performance Manual, The (Langfield)
Race & Trackday Driving Techniques (Hornsey)
Retro or classic car for high performance, How to modify your (Stapleton)
Rover V8 Engines, How to Power Tune (Hammill)
Secrets of Speed – Today's techniques for 4-stroke engine blueprinting & tuning (Swager)
Sportscar & Kitcar Suspension & Brakes, How to Build & Modify – Revised 3rd Edition (Hammill)
SU Carburettor High-performance Manual (Hammill)
Successful Low-Cost Rally Car, How to Build a (Young)
Suzuki 4x4, How to Modify For Serious Off-road Action (Richardson)
Tiger Avon Sportscar, How to Build Your Own – Updated & Revised 2nd Edition (Dudley)
TR2, 3 & TR4, How to Improve (Williams)
TR5, 250 & TR6, How to Improve (Williams)
TR7 & TR8, How to Improve (Williams)
V8 Engine, How to Build a Short Block For High Performance (Hammill)
Volkswagen Beetle Suspension, Brakes & Chassis, How to Modify For High Performance (Hale)
Volkswagen Bus Suspension, Brakes & Chassis for High Performance, How to Modify – Updated & Enlarged New Edition (Hale)
Weber DCOE, & Dellorto DHLA Carburetors, How to Build & Power Tune – 3rd Edition (Hammill)

RAC handbooks
Caring for your car – How to maintain & service your car (Fry)
Caring for your car's bodywork and interior (Nixon)
Caring for your bicycle – How to maintain & repair your bicycle (Henshaw)
Caring for your scooter – How to maintain & service your 49cc to 125cc twist & go scooter (Fry)
Efficient Driver's Handbook, The (Moss)
Electric Cars – The Future is Now! (Linde)
First aid for your car – Your expert guide to common problems & how to fix them (Collins)
How your car works (Linde)
How your motorcycle works – Your guide to the components & systems of modern motorcycles (Henshaw)
Motorcycles – A first-time-buyer's guide (Henshaw)
Motorhomes – A first-time-buyer's guide (Fry)
Pass the MoT test! – How to check & prepare your car for the annual MoT test (Paxton)
Selling your car – How to make your car look great and how to sell it fast (Knight)
Simple fixes for your car – How to do small jobs for yourself and save money (Collins)

Enthusiast's Restoration Manual Series
Beginner's Guide to Classic Motorcycle Restoration YOUR step-by-step guide to setting up a workshop, choosing a project, dismantling, sourcing parts, renovating & rebuilding classic motorcycles from the 1970s & 1980s, The (Burns)
Citroën 2CV, How to Restore (Porter)
Classic Large Frame Vespa Scooters, How to Restore (Paxton)
Classic Car Bodywork, How to Restore (Thaddeus)
Classic British Car Electrical Systems (Astley)
Classic Car Electrics (Thaddeus)
Classic Cars, How to Paint (Thaddeus)
Ducati Bevel Twins 1971 to 1986 (Falloon)
How to restore Honda CX500 & CX650 – YOUR step-by-step colour illustrated guide to complete restoration (Burns)
How to restore Honda Fours – YOUR step-by-step colour illustrated guide to complete restoration (Burns)
Jaguar E-type (Crespin)
Reliant Regal, How to Restore (Payne)
Triumph TR2, 3, 3A, 4 & 4A, How to Restore (Williams)
Triumph TR5/250 & 6, How to Restore (Williams)
Triumph TR7/8, How to Restore (Williams)
Triumph Trident T150/T160 & BSA Rocket III, How to Restore (Rooke)
Ultimate Mini Restoration Manual, The (Ayre & Webber)
Volkswagen Beetle, How to Restore (Tyler)
VW Bay Window Bus (Paxton)
Yamaha FS1-E, How to Restore (Watts)

Expert Guides
Land Rover Series I-III – Your expert guide to common problems & how to fix them (Thurman)
MG Midget & A-H Sprite – Your expert guide to common problems & how to fix them (Horler)
Essential Buyer's Guide Series
Triumph Herald & Vitesse (Davies)
Triumph Spitfire & GT6 (Baugues)
Triumph Stag (Mort)
Triumph Thunderbird, Trophy & Tiger (Henshaw)
Triumph TR6 (Williams)
Triumph TR7 & TR8 (Williams)

Great Cars
Austin-Healey – A celebration of the fabulous 'Big' Healey (Piggott)
Triumph TR - TR2 to 6: The last of the traditional sports cars (Piggott)

General
11/2-litre GP Racing 1961-1965 (Whitelock)
AC Two-litre Saloons & Buckland Sportscars (Archibald)
Alfa Romeo 155/156/147 Competition Touring Cars (Collins)
Alfa Romeo Giulia Coupé GT & GTA (Tipler)
Alfa Romeo Montreal – The dream car that came true (Taylor)
Alfa Romeo Montreal – The Essential Companion (Classic Reprint of 500 copies) (Taylor)
Alfa Tipo 33 (McDonough & Collins)
Alpine & Renault – The Development of the Revolutionary Turbo F1 Car 1968 to 1979 (Smith)
Alpine & Renault – The Sports Prototypes 1963 to 1969 (Smith)
Alpine & Renault – The Sports Prototypes 1973 to 1978 (Smith)
Anatomy of the Classic Mini (Huthert & Ely)
Anatomy of the Works Minis (Moylan)
Armstrong-Siddeley (Smith)
Art Deco and British Car Design (Down)
Autodrome (Collins & Ireland)
Autodrome 2 (Collins & Ireland)
Automotive A-Z, Lane's Dictionary of Automotive Terms (Lane)
Automotive Mascots (Kay & Springate)
Bahamas Speed Weeks, The (O'Neil)
Bentley Continental, Corniche and Azure (Bennett)
Bentley MkVI, Rolls-Royce Silver Wraith, Dawn & Cloud/Bentley R & S-Series (Nutland)
Bluebird CN7 (Stevens)
BMC Competitions Department Secrets (Turner, Chambers & Browning)
BMW 5-Series (Cranswick)
BMW Z-Cars (Taylor)
BMW Boxer Twins 1970-1995 Bible, The (Falloon)
BMW Cafe Racers (Cloesen)
BMW Custom Motorcycles – Choppers, Cruisers, Bobbers, Trikes & Quads (Cloesen)
BMW – The Power of M (Vivian)
Bonjour – is this Italy? (Turner)
British 250cc Racing Motorcycles (Pereira)
British at Indianapolis, The (Wagstaff)
British Café Racers (Cloesen)
British Cars, The Complete Catalogue of, 1895-1975 (Culshaw & Horrobin)
British Custom Motorcycles – The Brit Chop – choppers, cruisers, bobbers & trikes (Cloesen)
BRM – A Mechanic's Tale (Salmon)
BRM V16 (Ludvigsen)
BSA Bantam Bible, The (Henshaw)
BSA Motorcycles – the final evolution (Jones)
Bugatti Type 40 (Price)
Bugatti 46/50 Updated Edition (Price & Arbey)
Bugatti T44 & T49 (Price & Arbey)
Bugatti 57 2nd Edition (Price)
Bugatti Type 57 Grand Prix – A Celebration (Tomlinson)
Caravan, Improve & Modify Your (Porter)
Caravans, The Illustrated History 1919-1959 (Jenkinson)
Caravans, The Illustrated History From 1960 (Jenkinson)
Carrera Panamericana, La (Tipler)
Chrysler 300 – America's Most Powerful Car 2nd Edition (Ackerson)
Chrysler PT Cruiser (Ackerson)
Citroën DS (Bobbitt)
Classic British Car Electrical Systems (Astley)
Cobra – The Real Thing! (Legate)
Competition Car Aerodynamics 3rd Edition (McBeath)
Competition Car Composites A Practical Handbook (Revised 2nd Edition) (McBeath)
Concept Cars, How to illustrate and design (Dewey)
Cortina – Ford's Bestseller (Robson)
Coventry Climax Racing Engines (Hammill)
Daily Mirror 1970 World Cup Rally 40, The (Robson)
Daimler SP250 New Edition (Long)
Datsun Fairlady Roadster to 280ZX – The Z-Car Story (Long)
Dino – The V6 Ferrari (Long)
Dodge Challenger & Plymouth Barracuda (Grist)
Dodge Charger – Enduring Thunder (Ackerson)
Dodge Dynamite! (Grist)
Dorset from the Sea – The Jurassic Coast from Lyme Regis to Old Harry Rocks photographed from its best viewpoint (Belasco)
Dorset from the Sea – The Jurassic Coast from Lyme Regis to Old Harry Rocks photographed from its best viewpoint (souvenir edition) (Belasco)
Draw & Paint Cars – How to (Gardiner)
Drive on the Wild Side, A – 20 Extreme Driving Adventures From Around the World (Weaver)
Ducati 750 Bible, The (Falloon)
Ducati 750 SS 'round-case' 1974, The Book of the (Falloon)
Ducati 860, 900 and Mille Bible, The (Falloon)
Ducati Monster Bible (New Updated & Revised Edition), The (Falloon)
Ducati 916 (updated edition) (Falloon)
Dune Buggy, Building A – The Essential Manual (Shakespeare)
Dune Buggy Files (Hale)
Dune Buggy Handbook (Hale)
East German Motor Vehicles in Pictures (Suhr/Weinreich)
Fast Ladies – Female Racing Drivers 1888 to 1970 (Bouzanquet)
Fate of the Sleeping Beauties, The (op de Weegh/Hottendorff/op de Weegh)
Ferrari 288 GTO, The Book of the (Sackey)
Ferrari 333 SP (O'Neil)
Fiat & Abarth 124 Spider & Coupé (Tipler)
Fiat & Abarth 500 & 600 – 2nd Edition (Bobbitt)
Fiats, Great Small (Ward)
Fine Art of the Motorcycle Engine, The (Peirce)
Ford Cleveland 335-Series V8 engine 1970 to 1982 – The Essential Source Book (Hammill)
Ford F100/F150 Pick-up 1948-1996 (Ackerson)
Ford F150 Pick-up 1997-2005 (Ackerson)
Ford GT – Then, and Now (Streather)
Ford GT40 (Legate)
Ford Midsize Muscle – Fairlane, Torino & Ranchero (Cranswick)
Ford Model Y (Roberts)
Ford Small Block V8 Racing Engines 1962-1970 – The Essential Source Book (Hammill)
Ford Thunderbird From 1954, The Book of the (Long)
Formula 5000 Motor Racing, Back then ... and back now (Lawson)
Forza Minardi! (Vigar)
France: the essential guide for car enthusiasts – 200 things for the car enthusiast to see and do (Parish)
From Crystal Palace to Red Square – A Hapless Biker's Road to Russia (Turner)
Funky Mopeds (Skelton)
Grand Prix Ferrari – The Years of Enzo Ferrari's Power, 1948-1980 (Pritchard)
Grand Prix Ford – DFV-powered Formula 1 Cars (Robson)
GT – The World's Best GT Cars 1953-73 (Dawson)
Hillclimbing & Sprinting – The Essential Manual (Short & Wilkinson)
Honda NSX (Long)
Inside the Rolls-Royce & Bentley Styling Department – 1971 to 2001 (Hull)
Intermeccanica – The Story of the Prancing Bull (McCredie & Reisner)
Italian Cafe Racers (Cloesen)
Italian Custom Motorcycles (Cloesen)
Jaguar, The Rise of (Price)
Jaguar XJ 220 – The Inside Story (Moreton)
Jaguar XJ-S, The Book of the (Long)
Jeep CJ (Ackerson)
Jeep Wrangler (Ackerson)
The Jowett Jupiter - The car that leaped to fame (Nankivell)
Karmann-Ghia Coupé & Convertible (Bobbitt)
Kawasaki Triples Bible, The (Walker)
Kawasaki Z1 Story, The (Sheehan)
Kris Meeke – Intercontinental Rally Challenge Champion (McBride)
Lamborghini Miura Bible, The (Sackey)
Lamborghini Urraco, The Book of the (Landsem)
Lambretta Bible, The (Davies)
Lancia 037 (Collins)
Lancia Delta HF Integrale (Blaettel & Wagner)
Land Rover Series III Reborn (Porter)
Land Rover, The Half-ton Military (Cook)
Laverda Twins & Triples Bible 1968-1986 (Falloon)
Lea-Francis Story, The (Price)
Le Mans Panoramic (Ireland)
Lexus Story, The (Long)
Little book of microcars, the (Quellin)
Little book of smart, the – New Edition (Jackson)
Little book of trikes, the (Quellin)
Lola – The Illustrated History (1957-1977) (Starkey)
Lola – All the Sports Racing & Single-seater Racing Cars 1978-1997 (Starkey)
Lola T70 – The Racing History & Individual Chassis Record – 4th Edition (Starkey)
Lotus 18 Colin Chapman's U-turn (Whitelock)
Lotus 49 (Oliver)
Marketingmobiles, The Wonderful Wacky World of (Hale)
Maserati 250F In Focus (Pritchard)
Mazda MX-5/Miata 1.6 Enthusiast's Workshop Manual (Grainger & Shoemark)
Mazda MX-5/Miata 1.8 Enthusiast's Workshop Manual (Grainger & Shoemark)
Mazda MX-5 Miata, The book of the – The 'Mk1' NA-series 1988 to 1997 (Long)
Mazda MX-5 Miata Roadster (Long)
Mazda Rotary-engined Cars (Cranshaw)
Maximum Mini (Booij)
Meet the English (Bowie)
Mercedes-Benz SL – R230 series 2001 to 2011 (Long)
Mercedes-Benz SL – W113-series 1963-1971 (Long)
Mercedes-Benz SL & SLC – 107-series 1971-1989 (Long)
Mercedes-Benz SLK – R170 series 1996-2004 (Long)
Mercedes-Benz SLK – R171 series 2004-2011 (Long)
Mercedes-Benz W123-series – All models 1976 to 1986 (Long)
Mercedes G-Wagen (Long)
MGA (Price Williams)
MGB & MGB GT– Expert Guide (Auto-doc Series) (Williams)
MGB Electrical Systems Updated & Revised Edition (Astley)
Micro Caravans (Jenkinson)
Micro Trucks (Mort)
Microcars at Large! (Quellin)
Mini Cooper – The Real Thing! (Tipler)
Mini Minor to Asia Minor (West)
Mitsubishi Lancer Evo, The Road Car & WRC Story (Long)
Montlhéry, The Story of the Paris Autodrome (Boddy)
Morgan Maverick (Lawrence)
Morgan 3 Wheeler – back to the future!, The (Dron)
Morris Minor, 60 Years on the Road (Newell)
Moto Guzzi Sport & Le Mans Bible, The (Falloon)
Motor Movies – The Posters! (Veysey)
Motor Racing – Reflections of a Lost Era (Carter)
Motor Racing – The Pursuit of Victory 1930-1962 (Carter)
Motor Racing – The Pursuit of Victory 1963-1972 (Wyatt/Sears)
Motor Racing Heroes – The Stories of 100 Greats (Newman)
Motorcycle Apprentice (Cakebread)
Motorcycle GP Racing in the 1960s (Pereira)
Motorcycle Road & Racing Chassis Designs (Noakes)
Motorhomes, The Illustrated History (Jenkinson)
Motorsport In colour, 1950s (Wainwright)
MV Agusta Fours, The book of the classic (Falloon)
N.A.R.T. – A concise history of the North American Racing Team 1957 to 1983 (O'Neil)
Nissan 300ZX & 350Z – The Z-Car Story (Long)
Nissan GT-R Supercar: Born to race (Gorodji)
Northeast American Sports Car Races 1950-1959 (O'Neil)
Nothing Runs – Misadventures in the Classic, Collectable & Exotic Car Biz (Slutsky)
Off-Road Giants! (Volume 1) – Heroes of 1960s Motorcycle Sport (Westlake)
Off-Road Giants! (Volume 2) – Heroes of 1960s Motorcycle Sport (Westlake)
Off-Road Giants! (volume 3) – Heroes of 1960s Motorcycle Sport (Westlake)
Pass the Theory and Practical Driving Tests (Gibson & Hoole)
Peking to Paris 2007 (Young)
Pontiac Firebird (Cranswick)
Porsche Boxster (Long)
Porsche 356 (2nd Edition) (Long)
Porsche 908 (Födisch, Neßhöver, Roßbach, Schwarz & Roßbach)
Porsche 911 Carrera – The Last of the Evolution (Corlett)
Porsche 911R, RS & RSR, 4th Edition (Starkey)
Porsche 911, The Book of the (Long)
Porsche 911 – The Definitive History 2004-2012 (Long)
Porsche – The Racing 914s (Smith)
Porsche 911SC 'Super Carrera' – The Essential Companion (Streather)
Porsche 914 & 914-6: The Definitive History of the Road & Competition Cars (Long)
Porsche 924 (Long)
The Porsche 924 Carreras – evolution to excellence (Smith)
Porsche 928 (Long)
Porsche 944 (Long)
Porsche 964, 993 & 996 Data Plate Code Breaker (Streather)
Porsche 993 'King Of Porsche' – The Essential Companion (Streather)
Porsche 996 'Supreme Porsche' – The Essential Companion (Streather)
Porsche 997 2004-2012 – Porsche Excellence (Streather)
Porsche Racing Cars – 1953 to 1975 (Long)
Porsche Racing Cars – 1976 to 2005 (Long)
Porsche – The Rally Story (Meredith)
Porsche: Three Generations of Genius (Meredith)
Preston Tucker & Others (Linde)
RAC Rally Action! (Gardiner)
RACING COLOURS – MOTOR RACING COMPOSITIONS 1908-2009 (Newman)
Racing Line – British motorcycle racing in the golden age of the big single (Guntrip)
Rallye Sport Fords: The Inside Story (Moreton)
Renewable Energy Home Handbook, The (Porter)
Roads with a View – England's greatest views and how to find them by road (Corfield)
Rolls-Royce Silver Shadow/Bentley T Series Corniche & Camargue – Revised & Enlarged Edition (Bobbitt)
Rolls-Royce Silver Spirit, Silver Spur & Bentley Mulsanne 2nd Edition (Bobbitt)
Rover P4 (Bobbitt)
Runways & Racers (O'Neil)
Russian Motor Vehicles – Soviet Limousines 1930-2003 (Kelly)
Russian Motor Vehicles – The Czarist Period 1784 to 1917 (Kelly)
RX-7 – Mazda's Rotary Engine Sportscar (Updated & Revised New Edition) (Long)
Scooters & Microcars, The A-Z of Popular (Dan)
Scooter Lifestyle (Grainger)
SCOOTER MANIA! – Recollections of the Isle of Man International Scooter Rally (Jackson)
Singer Story: Cars, Commercial Vehicles, Bicycles & Motorcycle (Atkinson)
Sleeping Beauties USA – abandoned classic cars & trucks (Marek)
SM – Citroën's Maserati-engined Supercar (Long & Claverol)
Speedway – Auto racing's ghost tracks (Collins & Ireland)
Sprite Caravans, The Story of (Jenkinson)
Standard Motor Company, The Book of the (Robson)
Steve Hole's Kit Car Cornucopia – Cars, Companies, Stories, Facts & Figures: the UK's kit car scene since 1949 (Hole)
Subaru Impreza: The Road Car And WRC Story (Long)
Supercar, How to Build your own (Thompson)
Tales from the Toolbox (Oliver)
Tatra – The Legacy of Hans Ledwinka, Updated & Enlarged Collector's Edition of 1500 copies (Margolius & Henry)
Taxi! The Story of the 'London' Taxicab (Bobbitt)
Toleman Story, The (Hilton)
Toyota Celica & Supra, The Book of Toyota's Sports Coupés (Long)
Toyota MR2 Coupés & Spyders (Long)
Triumph Bonneville Bible (59-83) (Henshaw)
Triumph Bonneville!, Save the – The inside story of the Meriden Workers' Co-op (Rosamond)
Triumph Motorcycles & the Meriden Factory (Hancox)
Triumph Speed Twin & Thunderbird Bible (Woolridge)
Triumph Tiger Cub Bible (Estall)
Triumph Trophy Bible (Woolridge)
Triumph TR6 (Kimberley)
TT Talking – The TT's most exciting era – As seen by Manx Radio TT's lead commentator 2004-2012 (Lambert)
Two Summers – The Mercedes-Benz W196R Racing Car (Ackerson)
TWR Story, The – Group A (Hughes & Scott)
Unraced (Collins)
Velocette Motorcycles – MSS to Thruxton – New Third Edition (Burris)
Vespa – The Story of a Cult Classic in Pictures (Uhlig)
Vincent Motorcycles: The Untold Story since 1946 (Guyony & Parker)
Volkswagen Bus Book, The (Bobbitt)
Volkswagen Bus or Van to Camper, How to Convert (Porter)
Volkswagens of the World (Glen)
VW Beetle Cabriolet – The full story of the convertible Beetle (Bobbitt)
VW Beetle – The Car of the 20th Century (Copping)
VW Bus – 40 Years of Splitties, Bays & Wedges (Copping)
VW Bus Book, The (Bobbitt)
VW Golf: Five Generations of Fun (Copping & Cservenka)
VW – The Air-cooled Era (Copping)
VW T5 Camper Conversion Manual (Porter)
VW Campers (Copping)
You & Your Jaguar XK8/XKR – Buying, Enjoying, Maintaining, Modifying – New Edition (Thorley)
Which Oil? – Choosing the right oils & greases for your antique, vintage, veteran, classic or collector car (Michell)
Works Minis, The Last (Purves & Brenchley)
Works Rally Mechanic (Moylan)

Also available ... eBook Download now from www.digital.veloce.co.uk

Hubble & Hattie

BATTLE CRY!

Also available ... Apps Download now from www.digital.veloce.co.uk

www.veloce.co.uk

First published January 2007 by Veloce Publishing Limited, Veloce House, Parkway Farm Business Park, Middle Farm Way, Poundbury, Dorchester, Dorset, DT1 3AR, England. Fax 01305 250479/e-mail info@veloce.co.uk/ web www.veloce.co.uk or www.velocebooks.com. Reprinted March 2017.
ISBN: 978-1-787111-01-1 UPC: 6-36847-01101-7
© Martin Thaddeus and Veloce Publishing 2007 and 2017. All rights reserved. With the exception of quoting brief passages for the purpose of review, no part of this publication may be recorded, reproduced or transmitted by any means, including photocopying, without the written permission of Veloce Publishing Ltd. Throughout this book logos, model names and designations, etc, have been used for the purposes of identification, illustration and decoration. Such names are the property of the trademark holder as this is not an official publication.
Readers with ideas for automotive books, or books on other transport or related hobby subjects, are invited to write to the editorial director of Veloce Publishing at the above address.
British Library Cataloguing in Publication Data – A catalogue record for this book is available from the British Library.
Typesetting, design and page make-up all by Veloce Publishing Ltd on Apple Mac. Printed and bound by CPI Group (UK) Ltd, Croydon, CR0 4YY.

ENTHUSIAST'S RESTORATION MANUAL™

Classic Car Electrics

Tips, techniques & step-by-step repair, restoration & maintenance procedures

Martin Thaddeus

VELOCE PUBLISHING
THE PUBLISHER OF FINE AUTOMOTIVE BOOKS

Contents

Introduction 7	The vehicle circuit diagram 18	Battery life 33
The aim of this book 8	One circuit, many branches 18	**Battery maintenance** **33**
A little knowledge 8		External 33
Back to basics 8	**Chapter 5 – Magnetism &**	Internal 33
Range of models covered 8	**electricity** **20**	**Charging** **34**
Tools, equipment & workspace ... 9	The permanent magnet 20	**Jump-starting or booster-starting** ... **34**
	The electromagnet 20	Jump-start procedure 34
Chapter 1 – Safety **10**	The loudspeaker voice coil 20	Jump-starting with two batteries 35
	The solenoid 21	Jump-starter packs 35
Chapter 2 – Auto-electrics	The relay 21	**Battery handling and safety** **35**
– an overview **12**	Horn 21	Battery testing and the science bit... 36
Why do we need an electrical	The electric motor 22	Heavy discharge test 36
system? 12	The permanent magnet motor 22	Simple volt-meter readings 36
Let's look again at the starting		Hydrometer test 37
sequence 12	**Chapter 6 – Measuring current &**	The science in a nutshell 37
	diagnosis **23**	Discharge 37
Chapter 3 – Back to basics 1	The multi-meter 24	Charging 37
– basic electrical theory **15**	The live-tester 24	
"Electricity is the flow of electrons" .. 15		**Chapter 9 – Generator 1**
Simplified atoms 15	**Chapter 7 – The five systems** **25**	**– the DC dynamo** **38**
... and molecules 15	The battery 25	**Dynamo maintenance** **38**
Conductors 15	1. The charging system 25	**Bearings** **38**
... and insulators 16	2. The starter system 26	Brushes & commutator 39
Polarity and electron flow – +/- &	3. The ignition system 28	Cleaning 39
earth (ground) 16	4. The lighting system 29	**Testing** **39**
Earth (ground) 16	5. Accessories, ancillaries, or	Windings 39
	auxiliaries 30	Testing the dynamo output 39
Chapter 4 – Back to basics 2		Commutator care 40
– basic circuit theory & useful	**Chapter 8 – The battery** **31**	The voltage regulator/control box ... 41
information **17**	**How a battery works** **31**	Dismantling a dynamo 41
Amperage (I) 17	The lead-acid battery 31	Maintenance 42
Voltage (V) 17	Cells 31	Cleaning 42
Resistance (Ω) 17	Voltage 32	Checking & adjustment 42
Resistance rules 17	Capacity 32	Regulator check and adjust for a
Circuits 17	Battery casing 32	three bobbin regulator 43

CONTENTS

Regulator check and adjust for a two bobbin regulator................ 43
To check and re-set the cutout 43
Three bobbin 43
Two bobbin 43

Chapter 10 – Generator 2 – the AC alternator 44
Alternator construction 44
Alternator maintenance & servicing................................ 46
Replacing a dynamo with an alternator................................ 46
Control box and polarity change 46

Chapter 11 – The starter motor 47
Starting the engine 47
The inertia starter 47
Pinion stuck in mesh? 47
Inspect brushes & commutator 47
Removal 48
Cleaning the pinion & commutator.............................. 48
Fitting new brushes 50
Dismantling the motor 50
New brushes 50
Bushes... 50
Remove pinion 50
The starter solenoid 51
The pre-engaged starter motor 51
Removal from car 51
Cleaning the pinion set................... 52
Dismantling................................... 52
Dismantling the lever and pinion set... 52

The starter motor tests 52
In car tests.................................... 52
1. Battery................................... 52
2. Cables and connections 52
3. Volt-meter tests....................... 53
4. Starter motor out tests............. 53

Chapter 12 – The ignition system 54
The coil 54
How it works................................. 55
The distributor 55
The rotor-arm 56
The contact-breaker......................... 56
The HT leads 56

The sparkplugs................................. 56
The ignition tests.............................. 58
The HT leads and plugs 58
Contact-breaker............................... 58
Replacing the contact-breaker 59
Contact-breaker points gap 59
Timing the ignition........................... 59
Timing marks 59
Static timing 60
Dynamic timing with a stroboscope 60
Upgrading the ignition system........... 61
Contact-breakerless ignitions 61

Chapter 13 – Lighting........................ 63
The headlamps 63
Four headlamps? 65
Replacement of a sealed-beam unit..................................... 65
Semi-sealed units 65
Earlier headlamps 67
Stop, tail, and sidelights 67
Maintenance of brake and sidelamps............................... 68
Lights and the law............................. 68
Direction indicators or trafficators ... 69
Additional lamps 70
Spot or fog lamps 70
Reversing lights 70
Flashing indicators.......................... 71

Chapter 14 – Accessories 72
Essential accessories 72
The horn....................................... 72
The windscreen wipers................... 73
Heater fan.................................... 73
Non-essential accessories 74
Radio... 74
Electric washer pump..................... 75
Heated rear window....................... 75
Electric windows 76
Alarms and immobilisers 76

Chapter 15 – Instrumentation 77
The speedometer.............................. 77
Mileometer/odometer........................ 78
Tachometer or rev counter................ 78
Temperature gauge........................... 78
Petrol gauge 79

Ammeter 79
Oil pressure gauge 79
Mechanical type 79
Electrical type............................... 79
Clock 80

Chapter 16 – Wires, fuses & switches...................................... 81
Wiring.. 81
The loom/harness 81
Wire and cables 82
Colour codes and fault tracing........ 82
Stress fracturing and metal fatigue in wiring................................... 82
Connections.................................. 82
Screwed or bolted cable ends......... 82
Push-fit connectors........................ 82
Scotchlok..................................... 83
Shrink wrap 83
Insulating tape.............................. 83
Soldering 83
How to solder a connector to a wire 83
Method 1................................. 83
Method 2................................. 83
Earthing points.............................. 84
Fuse 84
Working with and around the loom....................................... 85
Replacing a front wing.................... 85
Typical RQP or mid-panel repair 86
Making up a section of loom – with thanks to Mike Wood at Frost 86
Loom swap................................... 86
Switches... 88
Manual switches............................ 88
Rotary variable switches 89
Other switch gear 89
Auto electrical cables and their applications (12V) 89
Contemporary guidebooks' recommended wiring................... 89
Modern metric cable specifications . 89
British Standard (BS) wiring colour codes 1986.............................. 89

Index.. 95

Enthusiast's Restoration Manuals from Veloce Publishing –

978-1-903706-44-2

978-1-903706-46-6

978-1-845840-93-8

978-1-845843-18-2

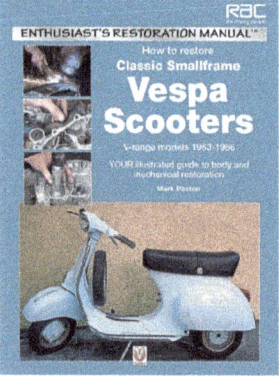
978-1-845844-37-0

978-1-845846-44-2

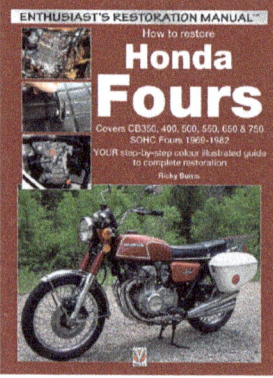
978-1-845847-46-3

978-1-845847-73-9

978-1-845848-82-8

978-1-845849-46-7

978-1-845849-47-4

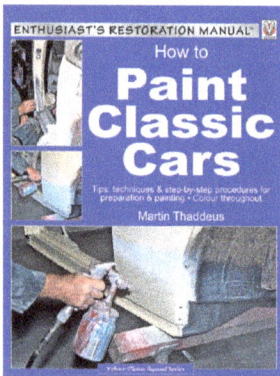
978-1-787111-42-4

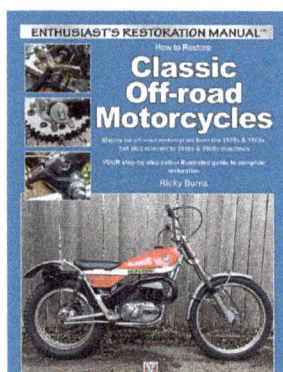
978-1-845849-50-4

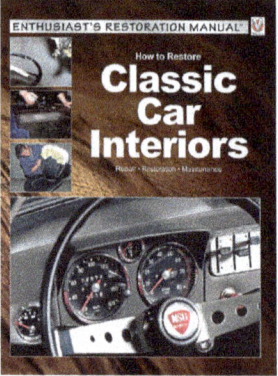
978-1-845849-83-2

978-1-787110-28-1

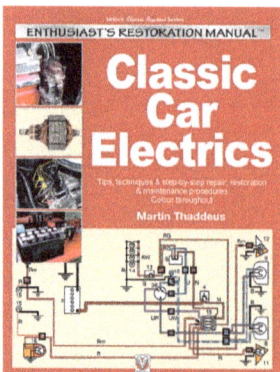
978-1-787111-01-1

Introduction

INTRODUCTION

One of the great attractions of older vehicles is that they speak to us of a simpler age – a time when technology was within the grasp of the man in the street. So many of the gadgets we employ in today's world are dependent on microelectronics and computerisation that we are in danger or becoming alienated from them; this is particularly evident when we consider the workings of the modern motor vehicle.

Open the bonnet (hood) of your new Ford Ciabatta or Audi Doodi – what can you see? Are any of the components readily recognisable? And if they are, can you, as the owner, service or replace any of them?

When my own Audi A1 took a hit, its 'brain' put the car into 'emergency drive mode', which in common parlance meant that it drove like a pig. I do, of course, accept that in doing so it may have protected some of its workings, and although resetting the ignition back to normal took my local main dealer a few minutes, it required a machine which cost more than the car is worth.

OK, how does this compare when we examine the business end of our '67 Anglia, E-Type, or Corvette Stingray? Usually this will present quite a different picture. In no time at all the familiar family of parts will reveal themselves – sparkplugs, distributor, coil, HT leads, starter motor etc – and all of them just waiting for us to rip them out and tinker with them on the kitchen table! And tinker we must, if we are to get the most from our beloved classics – for maintenance is the key to successfully running an older car.

Back in the days when many of our cars were current or simply 'a bit old',

A look inside modern Audi engine bays reveals ... nothing!

This lovingly maintained Herald reads like a text book. Which electrical components can you name at a glance?

ENTHUSIAST'S RESTORATION MANUAL SERIES

American muscle relies on familiar components.

The much-loved Ford 'Anglebox.'

This beautiful E-type has shiny goodies on display.

reliability and service intervals were very different to those which we know regard as normal. In almost any situation it was perfectly acceptable to excuse tardiness with the words "sorry, the car wouldn't start."

Similarly, up until the early eighties, it was not unusual for my neighbour to turn up on the doorstep of a morning asking for a bump-start; luckily we lived at the top of a hill. (Though, obviously, not so lucky if the damn thing didn't actually fire on the way down!)

By way of a comparison consider this ... Those of us who like to service our cars ourselves will probably think in terms of cleaning and gapping our sparkplugs on a yearly basis, whereas, according to my copy of The AA Book of the Car (which dates back to 1970), "most sparkplugs have a recommended service life of 10,000 miles; but it is advisable to remove, clean and refit them every 3000 miles – probably more often if the engine is in poor condition." To put it another way, at one-hundred thousand miles, yesterday's engine would be at the end of its life, while today's Cadillac would be due its first major service.

THE AIM OF THIS BOOK

As I have said, cars we know and love speak to us of technology that could be grasped by anyone. Simple electrics, such as we will be dealing with, require what is known as 'sequential logic' which is to say straight-forward reasoning. With an average tool-kit, a little bit of common sense, and this book, you should be able to tackle pretty much anything.

A LITTLE KNOWLEDGE ...

... is a very handy thing, and could save you a lot of grief! Here are two real life examples:

1. Many years ago I drove an Imp; it was a lovely little thing, but during a particularly cold spell became a bit temperamental. Sometimes it didn't want to start and other times it died for no apparent reason. One night I noticed sparking from the gear shift – what did this mean?

Answer. The 'earth strap', which returns the ignition voltage, had broken and so the current was taking any path it could back to the battery via the bodywork. A new strap cost me a couple of quid.

2. More recently, a friend of mine who runs a fleet of limousines was having trouble with an old Excalibur – this, in essence, is an '84 Lincoln town car. The problem was that the batteries kept going flat. I say 'batteries' because it features two huge units, which are located under the front wings and are a real pain to get to. After replacing the alternator at great expense and hassle, he then replaced the batteries and an external voltage/current regulator (which was part of the limo conversion). All of this was to no avail and the damn thing would not hold a charge.

Answer. The problem lay in the tiny little tell-tale lamp on the dashboard. It turns out that if the bulb (approx value – one peanut) is blown, then the whole charging circuit fails.

BACK TO BASICS

Should you not be familiar with electrics, fear not: I will assume no previous knowledge and, for the sake of clarity, I will go through the car system-by-system and component-by-component. If that still leaves you wondering, don't fret – I will start with basic electrical and circuit theory – atoms, molecules, electrons and the like.

RANGE OF MODELS COVERED

I have aimed this work at the owners of mass-produced cars from the fifties to the seventies, though any vehicle which relies upon 'electrics' as opposed to 'electronics' will be covered to some

INTRODUCTION

A live-tester is always my first weapon of choice when it comes to fault-finding.

Always use the correct tools when it comes to working with sparkplugs and the like. Skimping may prove costly.

extent. The information within the book could, for example, be used to service an eighties VW Golf or a thirties VW Beetle.

As the scope of what is termed a 'classic' is forever moving, no work can ever hope to cover everything. I have not attempted to get involved with fuel injection, as anything other than the very early systems will tend to be electronic – this is a book on 'electrics'.

Please note that any generic book can only give typical values when it comes to things like regulator, cut-off voltages or sparkplug gaps. I will distil the information from a variety of British classics and give you the salient points. Don't worry, you will easily make this book work for you.

TOOLS, EQUIPMENT & WORKSPACE

There is a dazzling array of tools and equipment on offer, and it is often tempting to think that it is all essential. In my experience, unless you intend to make a living as an auto-electrician, most of this stuff is to be purchased only as its need arises. Personally, I have always preferred the minimal approach. A simple live-tester with a built in lamp will allow you to trace if the power is where it should be; if it isn't, that tells you quite a lot, likewise if the power is there but things are still not working, then perhaps a simple multi-meter is called for. This can tell you if, for example, a generator is over- or under-charging.

A stroboscope type 'timing-light' is usually regarded as essential for servicing, and I would advise that you invest in a half-decent one. At a pinch even this can be worked around.

As well as your standard hand tools such as screwdriver and sockets, which are required to remove and install the components, you will need a few specialised items.

The other great essential is a place to work. For many years the spiritual home of the starter motor was on the kitchen table – alas, modern woman often looks darkly upon such practices, and so an alternative may have to be found. A flat, clean, well-lit area, which allows for screws and the like to be reserved before being refitted is essential. Tea making facilities would also be nice.

Chapter 1
Safety

SAFETY

Working with auto-electrics poses a number of risks to yourself and those around you. Some are obvious whilst others are not.

Please read the following before attempting to carry out any repair or maintenance to your vehicle.

I will endeavour to point out specific hazards as the book progresses, but for now here are a few things to take on board from the start.

1. **Electric shock.** The risk of electric shock is less of a problem than you might think; this is due to the relatively low 12 volts that the vast majority of the vehicle uses in its circuits. There is, however, one exception which does offer the opportunity to damage yourself in this manner: the ignition system – which can run at up to a whopping 30,000 volts – and, believe me, that can hurt! It also has the ability to jump across thin air and, being as you have to be in close proximity to a hot running engine in order to be 'zapped' by it, you run the risk of contacting the exhaust or fan as you recoil from the shock.

2. **Electrical burns.** Again, as most of the vehicle is powered by fairly low currents this is not a major concern, but there are exceptions to this rule: any conducting object, such as a spanner or screwdriver, that bridges any object which is live with any part of the body (which is an earth) will immediately cause a 'short'. I

Safety is a state of mind.

have seen spanners welded to inner wings due to inattentive mechanics. This is a particular problem when working near the battery, alternator or starter motor.

Again, the shock of shorting and the sparks which come with this may cause a person to jump – which in turn poses the risk of injury when working near hot or moving engine parts.

3. **Heat.** As we have just seen, a hot engine poses a risk to anyone working near it. Unfortunately, many of the components that we might wish to work with may also get hot whilst in use. These include

10

SAFETY

The battery is the heart of your system: a sound, clean and secure installation is essential.

headlights (which might not surprise you), and battery terminals (which often will). Soldering irons can also get pretty hot, and the fumes from the solder are noxious.

4. **Moving parts.** Pullies, fans, and belts are not nice things if your knuckles contact them. You'll need good lighting, good balance, and no loose clothing. And don't wear a watch.

5. **Live-testers and probes.** These are fitted with spikes and are often used in tight locations. Take care. They also carry the risk of shorting circuits out.

6. **Cars.** Working near and around motor vehicles is always hazardous. Whether on the floor, jacked-up, or in the street, keep your wits about you.

7. **Exhaust fumes.** As well as being noisy, vehicle exhausts are rather toxic – this goes double for older cars. Work in well-ventilated areas only.

8. **The battery.** The battery deserves its own cautionary note, due to its special place within the scheme of things. Please note:

A. Batteries are heavy and are often sited in the most awkward of places.
B. Batteries are filled with acid.
C. Batteries are stores of electricity which may spark violently.
D. Batteries are known to explode, showering anyone close by with burning acid.
E. Batteries may give off explosive and toxic fumes.

To my mind, the best defence when it comes to this type of work is the matter of your own mindset; I always tell people that I have to put on my 'electrical head'.

www.velocebooks.com/www.veloce.co.uk
All books in print • New books • Special offers • Gift Vouchers

Chapter 2
Auto-electrics – an overview

WHY DO WE NEED AN ELECTRICAL SYSTEM?

Imagine getting into your lovely old car – do you need an interior lamp? Insert the key and turn it to the first position. The radio might work – but the car is not going anywhere. Turn the key a little further and the second position is reached, at this point the ignition circuit is made live but still nothing really happens. Now, turn the key to its third position, after a 'clunk' the starter motor is activated. As the engine gathers speed, so fuel is drawn through the carb is be detonated in the cylinders. With the engine running under its own power, the starter falls out of mesh.

If you now release the key, the starter switch will return to the second position under the influence of a spring. As you drive off, you may employ a variety of lights. You might utilise the heater fan or you could find a need for the heated rear screen. The engine should now continue to run until the ignition system is shut down.

So, unless your vehicle is a crank-started diesel with acetylene lamps, obviously you will need electricity to run it.

Let's look again at the starting sequence

When you opened the door, a courtesy lamp came on; as the vehicle was not running the power to light this must have been provided from a battery. The lamp switch is hidden in the door shut and was of the plunger type, and probably has a single lead. If this is the case, then the bodywork acted as the other part of the circuit and returned the electrical current to the battery. The practice of utilising the metal bodywork in this way is the standard and saves an awful lot of wire.

A standard key switch shows the normal positions: 'lock' – steering lock; 'acc' (accessory) – radio, etc.; 'on' – normal running position; 'start' – engages the starter motor. A button is sometimes used for the last function.

AUTO-ELECTRICS – AN OVERVIEW

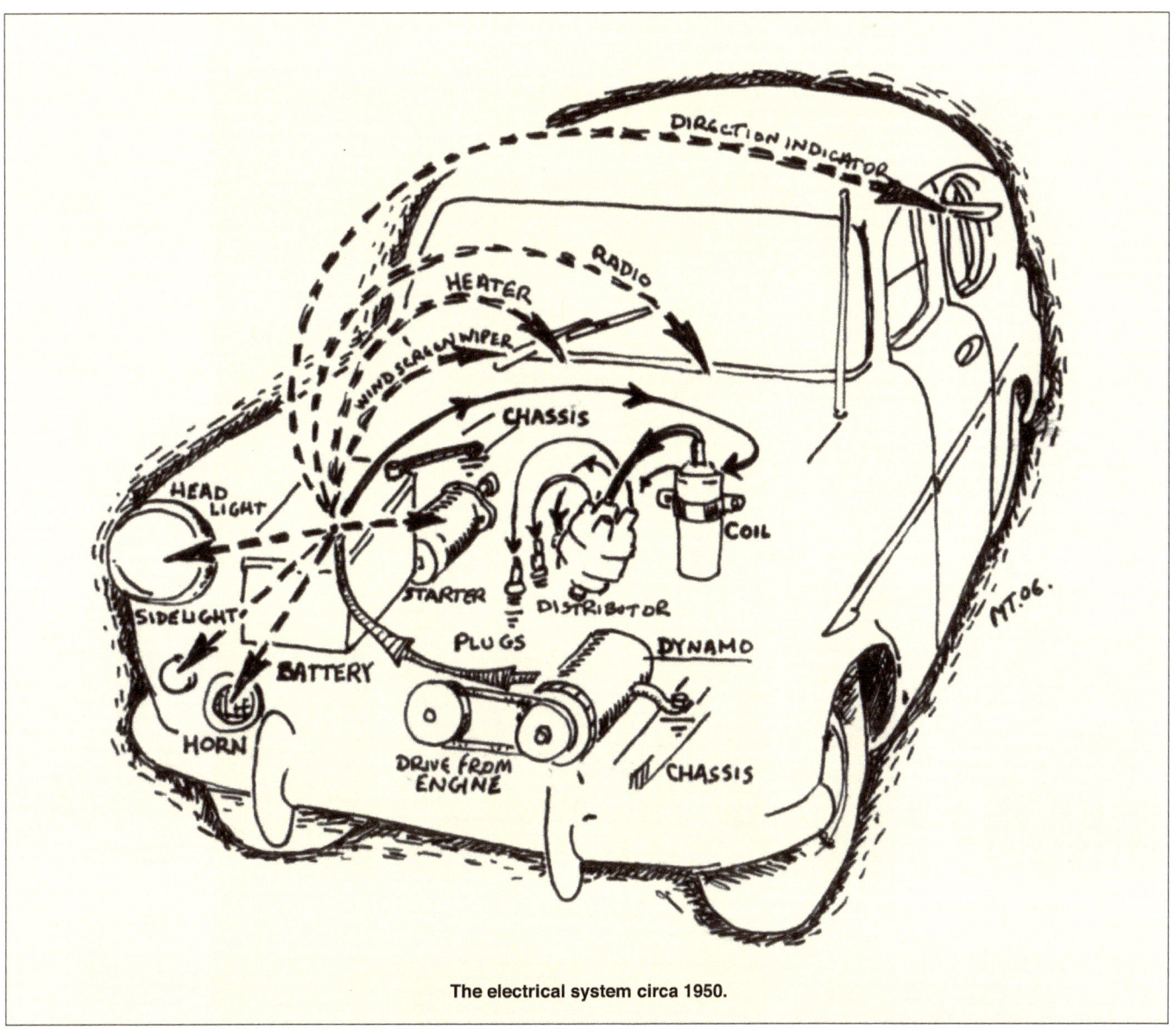

The electrical system circa 1950.

By turning the ignition switch to its first position, you have made it possible for auxiliary equipment such as a radio to be used without the engine running. This poses a risk of running down your battery, especially on vehicles fitted with a dynamo type generator as the reserve tends to be rather small.

On some cars the 'auxillary' position will be accessed by turning the key in the opposite direction, while others will feature some kind of '**détente**' or safety catch.

At its second position the switch powers up the igniton, i.e. the coil will be energised. The other components of the ignition system need to be in motion before they can have any effect. At the same time, a lamp on the dashboard will light – this may be labelled as 'ignition' or 'battery' or 'gen' (generator) and tells you that more power is being consumed than is being produced. In this condition or position, all of the car's electrical components should be usable, as this is the position of the key switch during normal running.

The final turn of the key against the spring will pass current to a solenoid which, in turn, connects the starter motor directly to the battery. The job of the solenoid is essentially that of a relay or electromagnetic switch – it allows a small current to control a larger one.

The current used to power the starter is pretty huge by car standards and it requires a very heavy cable. To keep this cable to a minimum, and to avoid bringing it up to the dashboard, the power from the key switch is used to close the solenoid only for the short time that the motor is actually needed. Some cars will also have an arrangement to divert power away from other circuits during the period when the starter is energised. The current is returned to the battery through the engine and, from here, via a cable which connects to the bodywork.

With the engine running (the key switch will be in its second position as before), your generator should now be producing enough power to run the ignition and any of the other systems fitted as standard to your vehicle. Earlier models will be fitted with a 'dynamo' – which is to say a DC generator. This type of unit is far less efficient than the later AC alternator, and may not be able to meet fully the demands with the engine idling, so a power supplement may have to be drawn from the battery.

The dynamo is also limited to a top

ENTHUSIAST'S RESTORATION MANUAL SERIES

speed of 6000rpm, beyond which it will not be able to cool itself effectively.

The ignition system is thought of as being divided into the HT (high tension/high voltage) and LT (low tension/low voltage). It also features so-called primary and secondary circuits – but don't worry too much about this terminology just yet.

The job of the coil is to provide a pulse of electricity that is able to jump the sparkplug gap in the form of a spark (no really!). In order to perform this task, the electricity has to be transformed from its normal 12 volts up to 60,000 volts or so.

The contact-breaker is located inside the distributor, and by opening and closing it diverts power at regular intervals to the coil which in produces the high voltage.

The distributor is turned by the engine. It derives its name from its job of distributing the power to the individual sparkplugs, which, in turn, ignite the fuel/air mixture. It performs this by means of a rotating contact.

While this combination of mechanical and electrical bits whizzing here and there might sound somewhat 'Heath Robinson', it is actually a very simple and elegant means of accurately igniting up to 200 charges per second, and that's in your simple four-pot engine. It's a system that has been around for a very long time. It is actually much easier to grasp the function of the ignition system when you have a motor vehicle in front of you.

On pulling away, you may have signalled your intention with a flashing lamp or, possibly, a semaphore type indicator. These will be operated by an electrical switch, which is usually on (or part of) a stalk at the side of the steering column.

The power to the direction indicators, as with many other systems, will also be controlled by the key switch. A flasher unit is also to be found in the indicator circuit and this may be considered a switch also: its job is to create the stop/start flashing of the lamps. The system will usually feature some kind of tell-tale lamp on the dashboard.

The speedometer, fuel gauge and oil pressure may also include some electrical component; the speedo might work independently of the battery system, while the other instruments will tend to run at relatively low powers.

When dealing with auto-electrical wiring from the time period we are interested in, we usually think in terms of a vehicle as having five distinct systems – these are:

1. Charging
2. Starting
3. Ignition
4. Lighting
5. Accessories

We can look at each of these in proper detail later, along with everything that we have just glanced at.

Put yourself behind the wheel.

Click ...

... click ...

... vroom!

"Yeah baby, here we go!"

www.velocebooks.com/www.veloce.co.uk
All books in print • New books • Special offers • Gift Vouchers

Chapter 3

Back to basics 1 – basic electrical theory

"ELECTRICITY IS THE FLOW OF ELECTRONS"

We are all familiar with the idea of atoms – these are the tiny weeny bits of matter which make up everything, everywhere. Atoms are made up of even smaller bits known as sub-atomic particles, and it is these which govern the differences between one kind of atom and another. For example, hydrogen has only one of each, and is the lightest and most plentiful substance in the universe, while helium has two of each and is correspondingly twice as heavy (though still jolly light!).

The particles themselves are divided into neutrons, protons and electrons, and each is thought of as having a different electrical charge: the neutron, as its name suggests, is neutral; the proton is positive; while the electron is considered as having a negative charge. There is no need to get a headache over this!

Simplified atoms ...

All atoms are similar in that the neutrons and protons make up a central nucleus, while the electrons orbit around them. The electrons are of the most interest to us.

Electrons orbit in what are sometimes called 'shells'; depending upon how many electrons an atom has, they will organise themselves into the respective layered shells and whizz around happily. The number of electrons in the outer shell seems to govern many of the characteristics of a substance and where that substance sits in the periodic table of elements. Again, don't worry too much about this.

... and molecules

Molecules are made-up of pairs or groups of atoms which share the odd electron. That is to say that instead of just orbiting their own nucleus, the electrons (or some of them) instead orbit the nuclei of neighbouring atoms.

Sharing electrons tends to result in very strong bonds between the atoms and if, for example, we could persuade the atoms which make up a molecule of water to split into loose atoms of hydrogen and oxygen, then the world's energy problems would be solved overnight.

Conductors ...

Some substances, notably many familiar metals, are considered as good conductors, that is to say that electrons can be persuaded to pass temporarily from one atom to the next. In order for this to happen we must apply a 'motive force' or 'voltage', which in layman's terms means that if we set up a situation where at one end of a conductor a deficit of electrons exists and at the other there is a surplus, then a flow of electrons will occur until the balance has been restored.

A simple example of this would be to place a wire between the two terminals of a battery. The pressure (voltage) would force the electrons to flow from one terminal toward the other through the wire until the balance was restored – at this point no voltage would exist and the battery would be 'flat'.

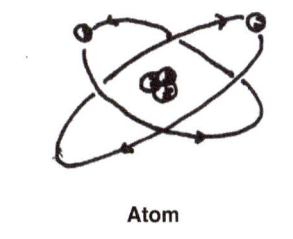
Atom

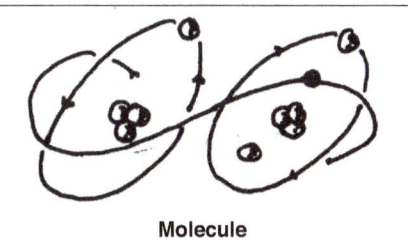
Molecule

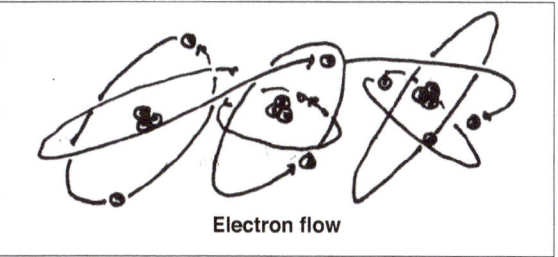
Electron flow

Silver is the best conductor available to us but its cost is prohibitive. Gold is pretty good and has the advantage of not oxidising (tarnishing) – gold is very popular for overpriced hi-fi connectors for this very reason but is only really suitable as a plating as it is rather soft. Copper and steel wires are the types that we will encounter most commonly; both of these metals are prone to oxidising, and this is always a consideration when working with electrical components.

Rust, verdigris, and other forms of metal oxide are poor conductors, and their formation on electrical contacts is the cause of many of the problems our cars face.

... and insulators

Materials which do not readily allow the flow of electrons are known as insulators, and we employ them to keep the electricity where we want it! In the absence of insulation, the current would tend to find the 'path of least resistance', i.e. the shortest or easiest route back to the battery. The path of least resistance is unlikely to be the most useful path – in fact, it would probably destroy, rather than run, our car.

Older vehicles will have wires which are bound with cotton and rubber, whilst more modern vehicles will tend to employ plastics such as vinyl (PVC). Very few classic car enthusiasts will wish to use original spec cable, most will prefer to employ a modern substitute.

Polarity and electron flow – +/- & earth (ground)

This next bit is going to cause a bit of confusion, but stick with me, as by getting it out of the way now we can proceed with greater clarity.

When we talk about electricity we use terms such as 'polarity', 'positive', 'negative', and 'earth' – what do these actually mean and what do we mean by them?

The positive terminal of your battery will have a deficit of electrons, while the negative will have a surplus. We understand the flow of electrons to be from positive to negative but, in fact, they flow the other way!

Earth (ground)

We understand that electrons flow away from positive and toward the negative although it actually goes the other way around, however, the convention remains and we work with the old idea although we know it to be wrong!

The Earth, as in the large ball that we live on, is capable of dissipating enormous electrical charges and is considered to be negative, as such, when we talk about returning the current to the battery after it has done its useful work, we often refer to this process as running the power to earth.

Where the vehicle's bodywork is used to return the current to the battery via its negative terminal, the system is said to be 'negative earth'. Conversely, if the current is returned through the body via the positive terminal this would be termed as 'positive earth'.

Vehicles manufactured before about 1970 are likely to have positive earth systems, and will probably be fitted with a DC dynamo type generator. Vehicles made after this time will most likely be of the negative earth type, and will almost certainly include an AC alternator as is still the standard today.

Many models whose life-spans ran through this time, will have begun life being produced with one polarity and ended it with the other. It is imperative that you are aware of the polarity of your particular model before attempting any electrical maintenance or alteration . Serious damage to the vehicle or yourself may occur due to incorrect wiring.

Positive and negative earth systems differ only in their polarity and neither is essentially better than the other. However, this does not mean that items designed to run on one standard can be used on the other. A radio, for example, which is designated as positive earth would have to be isolated from the bodywork of a negative earth vehicle in order to stop it shorting out.

A large number of cars which were originally built as positive earth, have subsequently been modified to negative earth and have been fitted with the more efficient AC type charging equipment.

As this was a common practice thirty-odd years ago, many purists will consider it a 'period' alteration, and as such acceptable.

Note – please be aware that, from now on, unless specified, I will assume a system to be 12V negative earth. Those of you with 6V or positive earth vehicles should not have any real problems translating the information in this book to your own particular application.

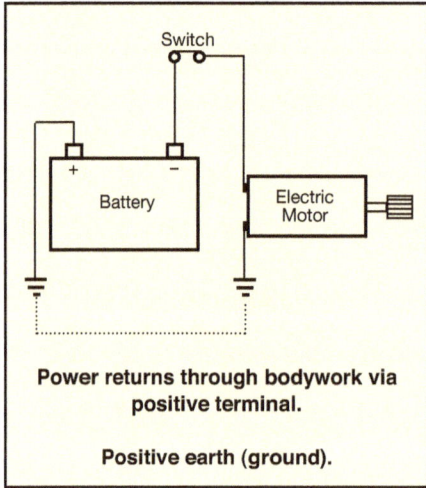

Power returns through bodywork via positive terminal.

Positive earth (ground).

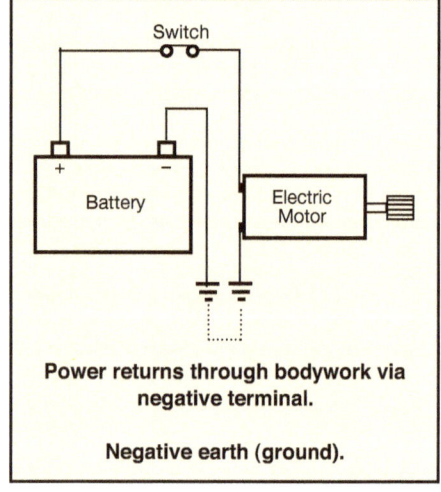

Power returns through bodywork via negative terminal.

Negative earth (ground).

Chapter 4

Back to basics 2 – basic circuit theory & useful information

"Electricity is the flow of electrons." This statement should now make sense to everyone, so let's take it a stage further.

AMPERAGE (I)

The flow or current of electricity is measured in amps or amperes (A); on diagrams it is also given the symbol 'I'.

One ampere is 6,240,000,000,000,000,000 electrons per second, which doesn't really trip off the tongue, so we tend to use 'amp' instead.

Smaller values of current flow are expressed as 'milli-amps' (mA) which is to say 0.001 amps = 1mA. It is not uncommon to find components with values in the range of 10s or 100s of milli-amps when dealing with motor vehicle electrical systems.

Larger wires are used to handle larger current flows; accordingly, the starter cable from the battery is usually the largest to be found on a normal road-going car – this may have to deal with a flow of up to 360 amps. At the other end of the spectrum, your fuel gauge requires only a tiny fraction of an amp, which is supplied by a correspondingly fine wire.

VOLTAGE (V)

The pressure or motive force which induces a current to flow is measured in volts (V). This voltage can be supplied from a battery or produced by a generator. In order for a flow to occur, the ends of a conductor must have a different voltage or, if you like, a 'voltage differential'.

Voltage is often compared to water pressure and in the same way as applying two equal pressures of water to a pipe would result in no flow across the pipe, by connecting two 12V supplies together we produce no current, but by applying this combined 'potential' to another conductor we might produce a flow with a pressure of 24V, as is the case with HGVs which use two 12V batteries.

RESISTANCE (Ω)

As we have seen, some materials readily allow the flow of electrons, while others will effectively prevent a flow. Between these two extremes exists a range of materials which are partially resistant to the flow, and which can be used as conductors or semi-conductors.

Our battery supplies a (more or less) constant 12V of pressure and we may have need to limit this; materials which have been put into a circuit to deliberately restrict the flow are termed 'resistors'.

We will sometimes have a need to vary the degree of resistance within a circuit. To this end we employ a 'variable resistor', also known as a 'potentiometer', e.g. a volume control or dimmer switch.

Resistance is measured in ohms (Ω), and the symbols used in diagrams are shown overleaf. Please note that the older rectangular symbol is identical to one of the earlier symbols used to denote a connector. Luckily we will not find too many of these particular components on pre-'70s vehicles.

RESISTANCE RULES

Everything has some resistance to electrical flow, there are no perfect conductors. If you double the length of any cable you will double its resistance to flow. If you double the cross-sectional size then resistance will be halved.

I have given a guide to wire thickness later in the book (see *Wiring*).

The properties of voltage, amperage, and resistance, will have a bearing upon each other. We will consider this shortly.

CIRCUITS

As you will have observed, the flow current is contained within a closed loop of conductors, starting with the positive terminal and ending at the negative: this is a circuit.

A basic circuit in which the power simply runs from the battery to a switch and on to a useful component before returning to the battery is called a 'series circuit'. A circuit in which the power diverges and feeds more than one component at once is called a 'parallel circuit'. The switch can be placed at any point within the circuit as any break in the continuity of the conductors would prevent the current from flowing.

Circuits can, of course, be far more

ENTHUSIAST'S RESTORATION MANUAL SERIES

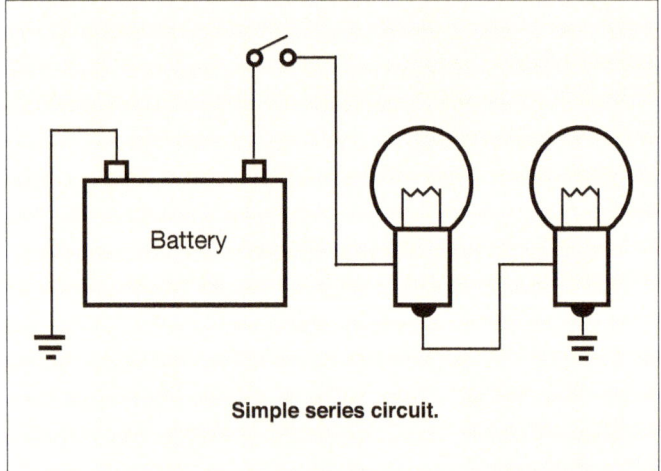

Simple series circuit.

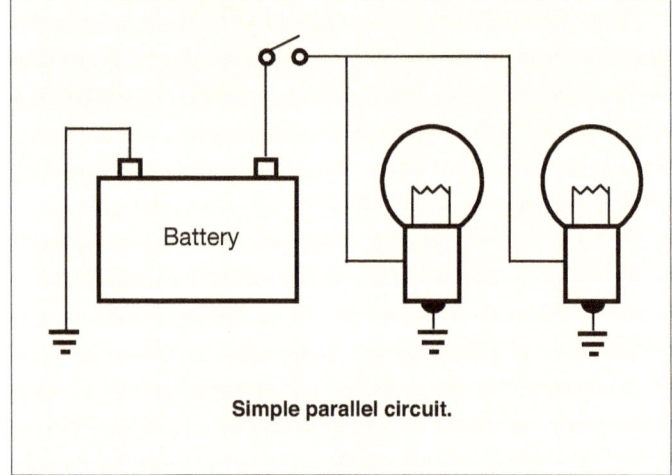

Simple parallel circuit.

complicated than the ones so far looked at; many of the systems that we will encounter within our vehicles will feature more than one switch and may, in fact, split to feed more than one component. Lighting circuits, for example, will feature 'parallel' feeds to the lamps which originate from a common switch – these may or may not then run to separate earth points on the bodywork.

The advantage of the parallel circuit in relation to lamps is two-fold: if a series layout were to be adopted, i.e. with one lamp fed before the other, then the first lamp would tend to cause the second to shine less brightly, as the inherent resistance within the first unit would impede the voltage to the second. The other drawback would become apparent if the first bulb 'blew'. This would result in no power flowing to the second lamp.

Another feature you will encounter, notably in the ignition system, is that a circuit may have a primary and secondary element in which the primary is of low voltage and the secondary a great deal higher.

These sides of the circuit may be considered separately to some extent, but as they are dependent on each other must also be thought of as a whole.

The vehicle circuit diagram

Take a look at the simplified circuit diagram I have supplied, and you will see that some areas have been set aside for clarity at the expense of 'geographical' accuracy.

Most manufacturers' circuit diagrams attempt to start at one end of the vehicle and finish at the other. Note how in this example the fuses appear to be dotted across the car at random when in fact they are located side by side in a little box.

You may also have noticed that many diagrams make no mention of colour. Unfortunately, even now there is no convention on colour coding for auto-electrical wiring, even after one-hundred years of car production. Even within a single manufacturer little consistency can be found, some models even feature entire looms where every single wire is black.

When trying to comprehend a particular circuit or system it is sometime useful to draw a schematic of that circuit in isolation. It will also pay dividends to look at the real components in situ, and to then relate them to the diagram as it appears in front of you.

One circuit, many branches

We often talk in terms of the different circuits and systems of the vehicle, but as they all originate and terminate at the same points, you might also consider the entire electrical system as one large complicated circuit with many branches. This would be correct, but it would also cause you quite a headache – so we wont!

We will look at the manner in which the different circuits are separated in a later section.

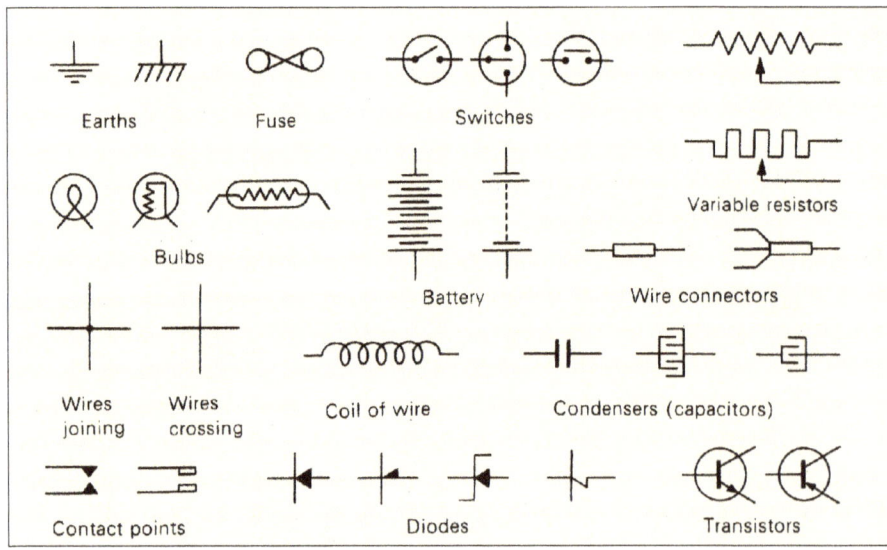

Key to typical wiring diagram circa 1960.

Opposite: Typical wiring diagram for a saloon circa 1960.

BACK TO BASICS 2 – BASIC CIRCUIT THEORY & USEFUL INFO

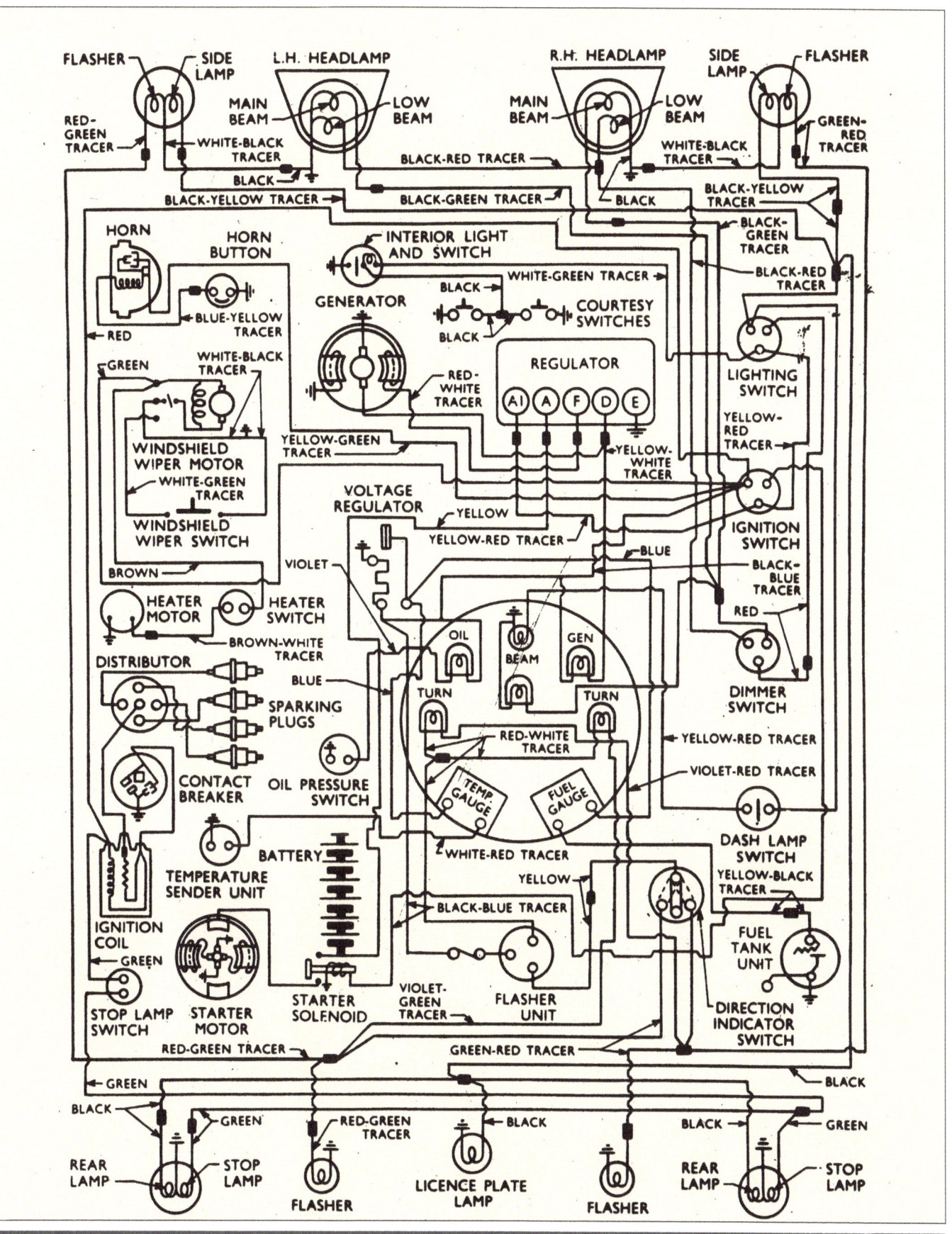

Chapter 5
Magnetism & electricity

The phenomenon of magnetism is inextricably linked to our understanding of electricity. We utilise the power of magnets to generate electricity and then reverse the same effect in order to turn a motor. Many of the electrical components found in even the most basic motor vehicles rely on the interaction of electricity and magnetism. As well as the more obvious moving parts, magnetism is also responsible for the workings of the ignition coil. I will explain ...

Whenever a current flows through a wire it will produce a magnetic field: usually this is of no great importance. Should the wire in question be wound into a coil, the magnetic field will tend to impede the flow of electrons, and will also have the effect of concentrating the magnetic properties – thus we have a simple electromagnet. This electromagnet is greatly enhanced in its effect if we then place a piece of material, such as soft iron, within the coil which will become temporarily magnetised.

Now consider this: if the same coil of wire has no current flowing through it and we move a magnet through the centre of the coil, a current will tend to be 'induced' in the wire.

THE PERMANENT MAGNET
The common magnets which we are all familiar with (like the ones on your fridge) are essentially bits of iron alloy which have been persuaded to have a lot of the metal crystals aligned in one direction. By lining up the crystals it is easier for some of the electrons to flow around the magnet in a coherent manner. This, in turn, means that the magnetic field generated by the flow of electrons is also more coherent and therefore concentrated.

Magnets are thought of as having two 'poles', and the magnetic flux will flow between these. The lines of flux exit via the north pole, and, after flowing through some of the surrounding matter, are drawn back into the magnet at the south pole. You will, of course, notice that the Earth has similar features, and also has a substantial iron mass inside it.

It is accepted that similar poles of different magnets will repel each other, while opposite poles will always attract – the label 'north' is given to the magnet's pole because of the attraction of the north pole of a magnetic compass to the North Pole of the earth – "So shouldn't that be 'south'?"

THE ELECTROMAGNET
By winding a coil around a piece of so-called 'soft iron', we can produce a very powerful magnet which can be controlled at the flick of a switch. Soft iron has the property of being able to return to a non-magnetic state, when the current is switched off.

THE LOUDSPEAKER VOICE COIL
Though not strictly an auto-electrical component, the workings of a simple

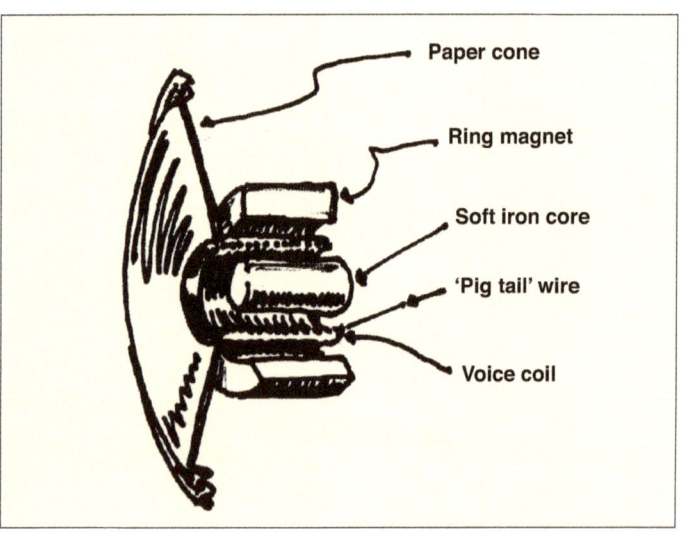

The mechanics of a speaker.

MAGNETISM & ELECTRICITY

loudspeaker neatly illustrate the principles of the electromagnet and its relationship with both soft-iron and the permanent magnet.

The basic speaker works by moving air in a fashion which mimics the original sound that has been recorded. A signal from the amplifier is supplied in the form of a series or electrical pulses and waves which fluctuate in strength (amplitude), frequency (pitch), and polarity.

The voice coil of the speaker is attached to the speaker cone, in such a way that it is suspended both inside a ring-magnet and surrounding a core of soft-iron. A signal passing in one direction (a current of one polarity) causes a movement in one direction, while a current in the other direction will effect a movement in the other.

THE SOLENOID

By comparison with the speaker coil, the solenoid is quite brutal, but it works by the same principle.

The simple solenoid consists of a spring-loaded plunger which, if depressed, would close the contacts of a high-power electrical switch. Typically this switch is in-line between the battery and starter motor.

The solenoid plunger is suspended within an electromagnet and, when this is energised, it causes the plunger to be drawn inward. This, in turn, closes the switch contacts, allowing current to pass through. When the electromagnet is switched off, so too is the high-power circuit supplied from the solenoid.

More sophisticated solenoids will feature a 'pull-down coil', and a 'hold-down coil'. Most vehicles which feature this type of 'remote-starter' solenoid, allow the owner to spin-over or start the engine by simply depressing the plunger manually. This should not be the case with automatic vehicles.

Solenoids are available to handle any power rating you might need on a car or truck. Later vehicles will feature a starter solenoid which is built into the motor assembly. This type of starter motor is known as pre-engaged, as well as its job as detailed above, the solenoid performs the function of positively placing the drive pinion in and out of mesh.

THE RELAY

The simple relay is a solenoid in minature, it is sealed in a tidy little box. As its size suggests, the relay is not designed to handle huge powers, the most common application for this device to the enthusiast is when fitting items such as heated rear windows or upgraded lighting.

HORN

The horn works on a similar principle to the relay, in that a magnetic effect is used to control a switch. In this case, though, when the horn button is pressed, the current energises a coil that attracts a soft iron core, which is attached to a diaphragm. As the core is pulled toward the coil, it lifts another set of contacts which break the circuit, causing the magnetic field to collapse. The diaphragm then springs back to its start position and the cycle is repeated until the horn button is no longer pressed. By this method a note is produced. Note – most vehicles will feature two horns or differing notes.

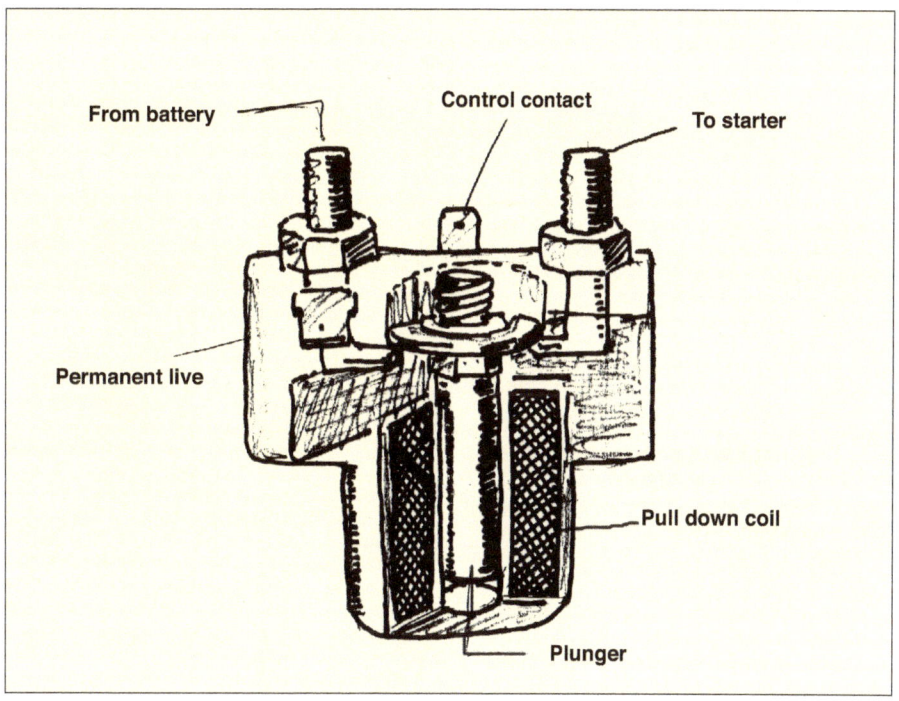

Inside the solenoid.

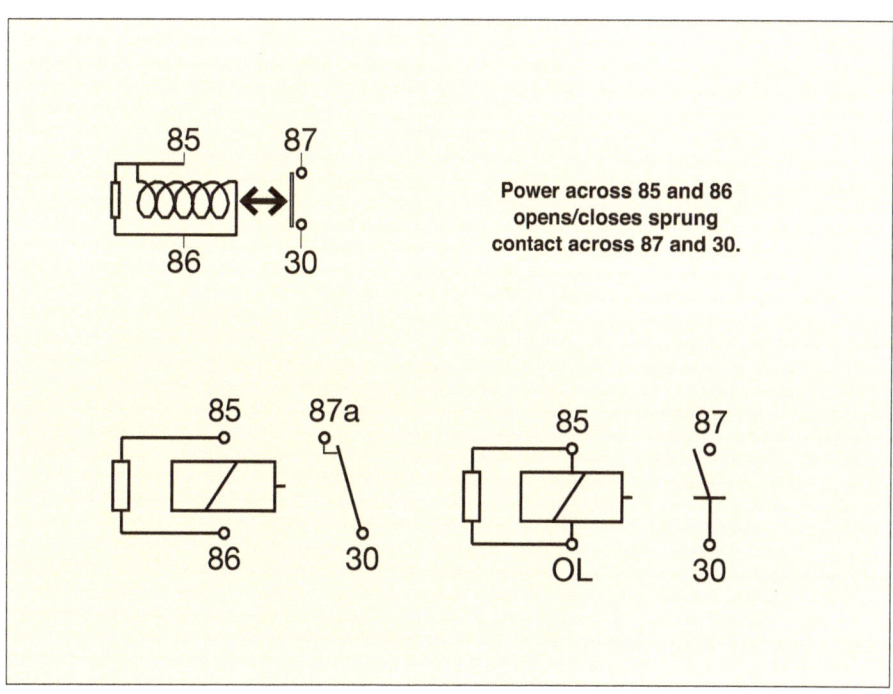

Typical relay circuits with terminal numbers.

Power across 85 and 86 opens/closes sprung contact across 87 and 30.

ENTHUSIAST'S RESTORATION MANUAL SERIES

THE ELECTRIC MOTOR

Any electric motor works on the principle that the similar of poles of magnets will repel each other, while the opposite poles will attract. By setting up magnets around a rotor which is itself made of electromagnetic coils, we can persuade the rotor to move toward a position where the magnets are balanced and stable. If we then switch the polarity of the rotor coils we can induce the rotor to continue turning.

By repeated switching of the coils which are built into the central rotor, through the commutator which supplies them, we can make the rotor spin until the current is cut.

THE PERMANENT MAGNET MOTOR

The motorised toys you had as child will all have included a motor of the permanent magnet type. As the name suggests, the magnets that turn the rotor when the rotor coils were energised are of the permanent variety. You will probably recall how turning this type of device by hand met with some resistance. In the permanent magnet motor, only the armature (rotor) windings are fed with current.

In the main, electric motors used for auto electric applications will be of the electromagnet type, however, the permanent magnet has now been sufficiently improved that it will be found

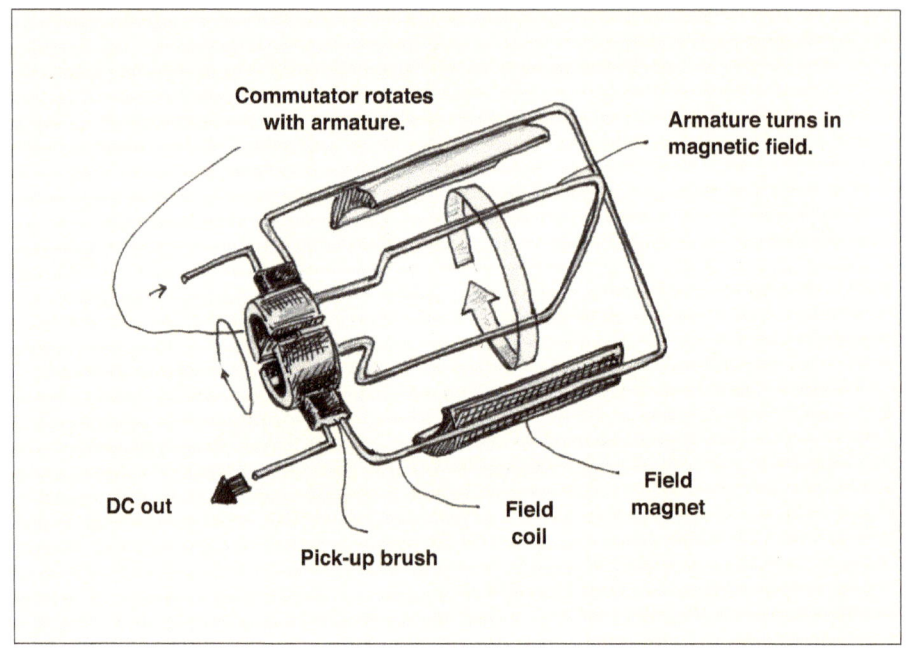

A simplified electric motor.

in many newer cars for such jobs as lifting door windows or power hoods.

Electromagnet type motors come in two varieties known as 'series' and 'shunt'; a third type known as 'compound' is a hybrid of the two. The series motor derives its name from the fact that the field (magnet) coils and the armature (rotor) are fed in series – that is to say, the power flows through one and then the other. The shunt motor differs in that the field coils are fed in parallel with the armature.

www.velocebooks.com/www.veloce.co.uk
All books in print • New books • Special offers • Gift Vouchers

Chapter 6
Measuring current & diagnosis

An obvious property of electricity is that we cannot actually see it. We can, however, measure it. More importantly, we can detect and measure the different properties that we have already covered.

Amperage can be measured with an ammeter (amp-meter). As amperage is the flow of electricity, it is necessary to place the meter in the circuit and have the flow of electrons pass through the meter itself.

In order that the act of measuring does not unduly impede the circuit in question, the meter must not resist the flow to a measurable extent. Likewise, if the meter is used to run the current away from the component, its measurement will be meaningless.

Having seen the size of cable required to handle the maximum amperage demanded by the starter, it should be apparent that the average domestic ammeter is not going to be able to cope with measuring that sort of power – and it doesn't have to. By measuring the voltage of a particular component such as the battery or generator, we can usually ascertain its state of health.

Voltage can be measured with a voltmeter. As some of the pressure or voltage is lost due to resistance within any component, it is often useful to measure the voltage at different stages of a circuit. Voltage can also be measured across a component to gauge a 'voltage drop'. If no voltage can be found in a circuit or in part of a circuit when a potential exists, then the full voltage must be blocked somewhere along the line.

By touching the red probe from the meter to a point which is live, and the black probe to earth, you can quickly detect where the blockage, leak or break in continuity lies.

In order to measure voltage, it is not necessary to place the meter directly in circuit – rather the meter is usually placed in parallel 'across' the area to be measured. Again, a good meter must use very little current if it is to produce useable results.

Resistance is measured with an ohmmeter. Resistance is relative to current flow and voltage, and so in order to measure it objectively the ohmmeter passes a current of a known voltage through the component or circuit in question and then measures the current as it returns. Any loss of current must be a measure of resistance within the item being metered.

The power for the resistance check is supplied from the ohmmeter's internal battery, and to perform this test the component or circuit in question must be isolated from any other conducting material.

It is often the case that the correct resistance value of a component is not known, but the same test is still of great value when continuity is in question. For example, a bulb filament may appear to be intact, but if no reading can be obtained for resistance, then it is doubtful a complete circuit exists within the structure.

You cannot see electricity, but you can measure its properties.

ENTHUSIAST'S RESTORATION MANUAL SERIES

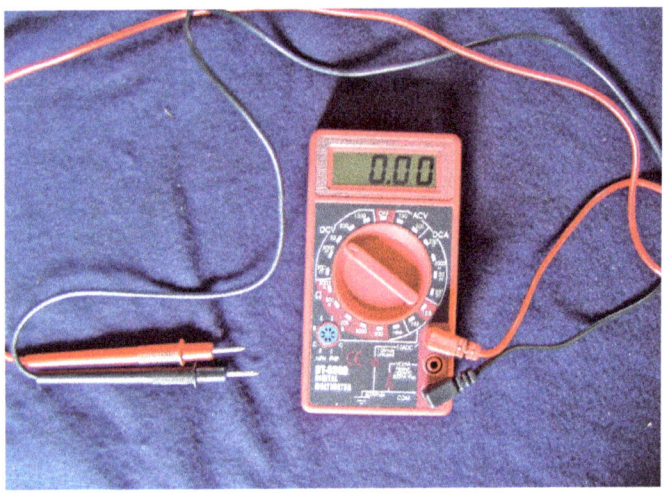

Multi-tester and leads.

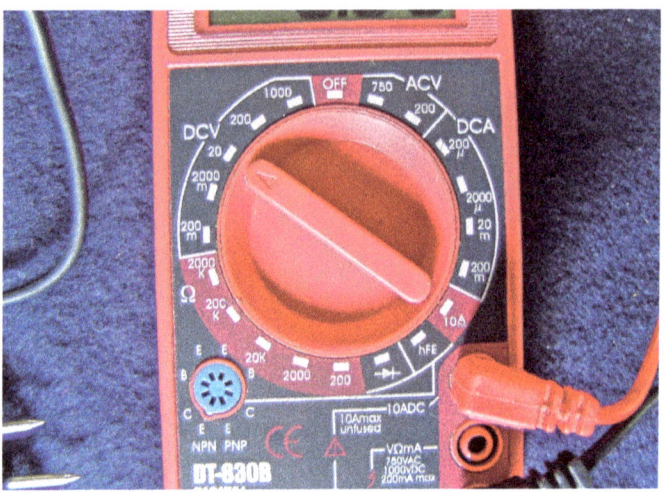

A closer look reveals the ranges of the meter.

THE MULTI-METER

As its name suggests, the multi-meter is a meter which can perform a multitude of tasks. The little unit pictured here is as basic as they come, and cost only about as much as a pint of beer! This one is of the digital variety and has ranges for resistance, DC voltage, and DC amperage. It will also check out transistors, diodes and the mains. Diodes are found in the alternator regulator, so this may be of use to someone!

A huge variety of multi-meters are available, and some are dedicated to the diagnosis of auto-related problems. For a little more money you can have a device which can also analyse your ignition and dwell angle – very tasty!

A closer look at my little multi-meter will reveal that the amp side can only handle powers up to 200mA, which isn't enough power to light a small bulb, let alone turn the engine over. In truth, the only time that an ammeter is of real use to us is in order to measure the output of the generator.

It is not feasible that anyone is going to purchase a 50 amp ammeter solely for this job, so we will work around that.

Naturally, as we look at the different systems and components of the motor vehicle, I will show you how best to utilise the multi-meter and consider any sensible options. Such as ...

THE LIVE-TESTER

The humble live-tester is basically a lamp, which is fitted between a metal spike and an earth lead. By attaching the lead to a known earth point, and then waving the spike around a bit, any live areas that this probe contacts will cause the lamp to light up. Warning! – don't wave a live-tester or anything else around an engine while it is running, as this may result in some serious injury or damage.

This very simple device is always my weapon of choice when it comes to diagnosing electrical faults. So many of the problems associated with older vehicles are due to faulty, or simply dirty, connections; by tracing where the power is, we can often see why it isn't where we want it to be! More of this later.

We will now consider some of the properties of electricity, and how they relate to the motor vehicle. In particular we will look at the diagnosis of circuit and component faults.

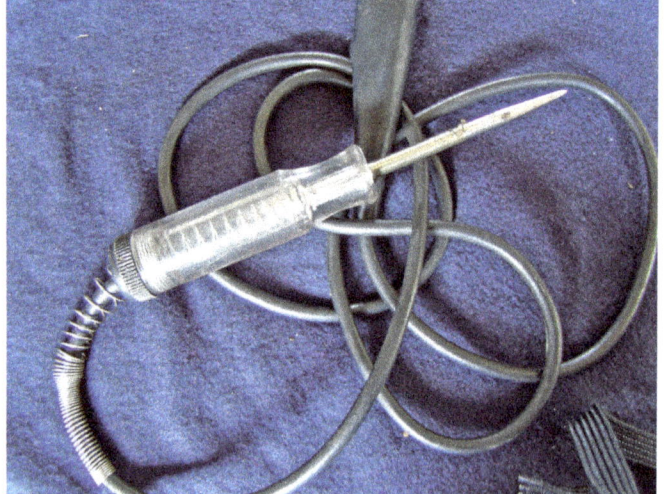

The simple live-tester is a lamp, a spike and an earth lead ...

... but its uses are endless when it comes to diagnosis.

Chapter 7
The five systems

The electrical system of any vehicle can be considered as a whole, but it is usually easier to subdivide it into the five systems described below:

1. Charging
2. Starting
3. Ignition
4. Lighting
5. Accessories

Many of the cars that we will be dealing with will actually be wired in such a way as to physically separate the circuits in this manner.

Before we go any further I want to draw your attention once more to the role of the battery ...

THE BATTERY
The battery is central to every circuit and system within the car, as such it is usually the first place to check, regardless of where any actual problem appears within the vehicle.

It is also imperative that you never attempt to run your vehicle without a suitable battery being in circuit. Your battery is the reservoir of electricity and also the buffer which protects all of your systems from voltage and current fluctuations which might be produced by the generator.

Failure to keep the battery terminals clean and secured will render any other maintenance virtually redundant.

The systems are:

1. THE CHARGING SYSTEM
The charging system consists of the battery, a control box, and the generator, along with a tell-tale light on the dash.

Earlier vehicles with DC dynamo systems will feature a separate control box, which is usually sited on the bulkhead. The job of the control box is to regulate the current and to protect the electrical system as a whole.

A tidy battery installation with clean, well-secured terminals.

ENTHUSIAST'S RESTORATION MANUAL SERIES

Dynamo in situ: a long-lived DC generator in classic tractor.

Alternator in situ: this E-Type has been upgraded – note the heat shield.

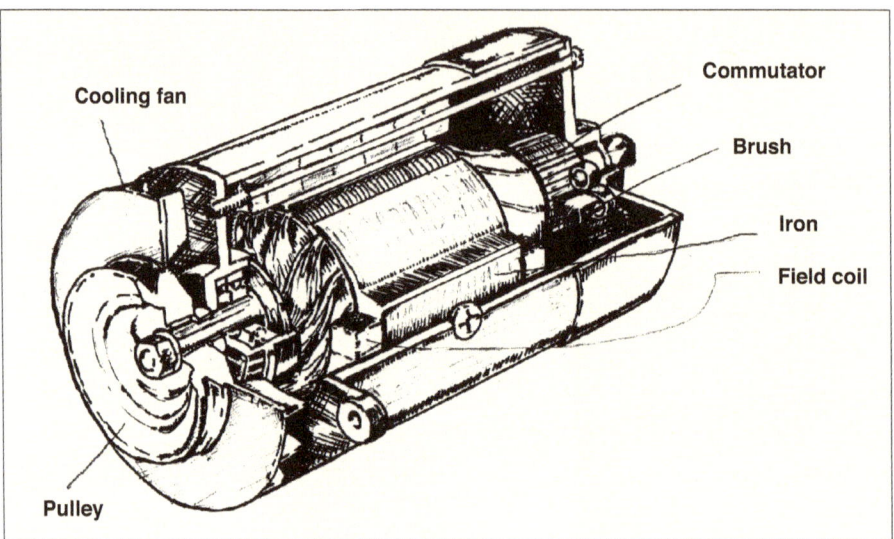

Dynamo.

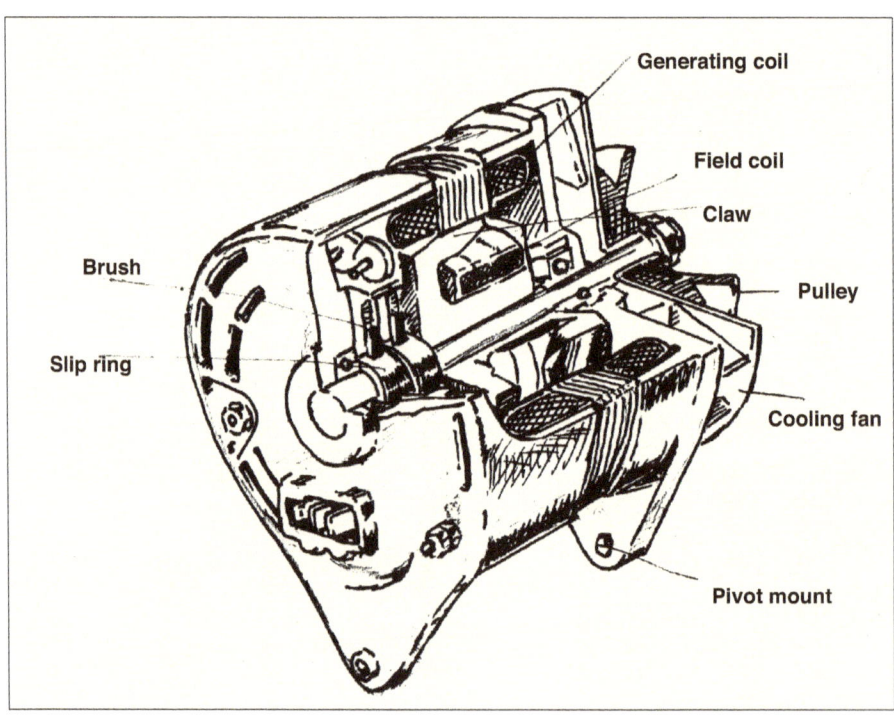

Alternator.

At low revs the dynamo does not turn fast enough to generate power, and in this state may draw power from the battery and act as a motor. To prevent this happening, the power to the dynamo is cut until the speed builds up.

In order for the dynamo to generate power, its field coils need to be fed from the battery, and the supply of this current is governed by the control box. At increased speed the dynamo will supply power to feed itself.

The voltage regulator/control box may or may not be adjustable, either way it will have been preset at the factory. We are usually limited to cleaning or replacing this item. Control boxes which are adjustable often require a special tool, and the specifications of the individual unit will be needed before any work is carried out.

Later AC alternator systems will usually have the voltage regulator/control system built into the alternator itself. In this type of system – which is now the norm – the regulator not only controls the amount of power, but also has the job of 'rectifying' the AC alternating current produced by the generator into DC direct current which can be used by the battery.

The control circuits are not user-serviceable.

The field coils may, in fact, be fed through a tell-tale lamp fitted on the dashboard at low outputs, and failure of this bulb may result in failure of the entire charging system.

The electonics built into the alternator's control system may be damaged by the use of a MIG welder – if a surge protector is not fitted across the battery – it's safer to disconnect the battery.

2. THE STARTER SYSTEM

The starting system consists of the battery and the starter motor, along with the starter-solenoid, ignition switch, and the cables which link them. Automatic vehicles will also have an inhibitor switch fitted to the gearbox to prevent accidental starting of the car whilst it is in gear.

I have made a particular point of including the wiring as a part of this system because the role of the actual cable is critical to successful starting of the engine, and also a common source of problems.

The starter motor is essentially a heavy-duty electric motor with a cog on the

THE FIVE SYSTEMS

Inertia starter motor.

Solenoid in situ.

Solenoid on bench.

end of it. It is used to turn over the engine from rest until it is spinning fast enough to draw fuel in a manner which can be detonated effectively. Most of the vehicles that we are interested in will need the engines rotated to about 50rpm to get them going. On a cold winter's morning, when the oil is thick, the starter might demand as much as 360 amps – enough to drain a fully charged battery in minutes.

Starter motors come in two varieties: firstly the inertia or Bendix type in which the driving pinion or cog is drawn into mesh with the flywheel by inertia (no really!) and the solenoid is a separate unit; secondly we have the pre-engaged type, in which the solenoid is fixed to the motor body and is used to push the starting pinion into mesh.

It is imperative that we deliver the power to the starter motor in as efficient a manner as possible; to this end the cable runs directly from the battery to the motor, is of very thick construction, and is broken only at the solenoid. The voltage to actuate the solenoid is supplied from the ignition switch, and will not be fused.

Starter cable is usually made of insulated copper, and is of a heavier gauge than any other sheathed wire. The

Inertia starter motor.

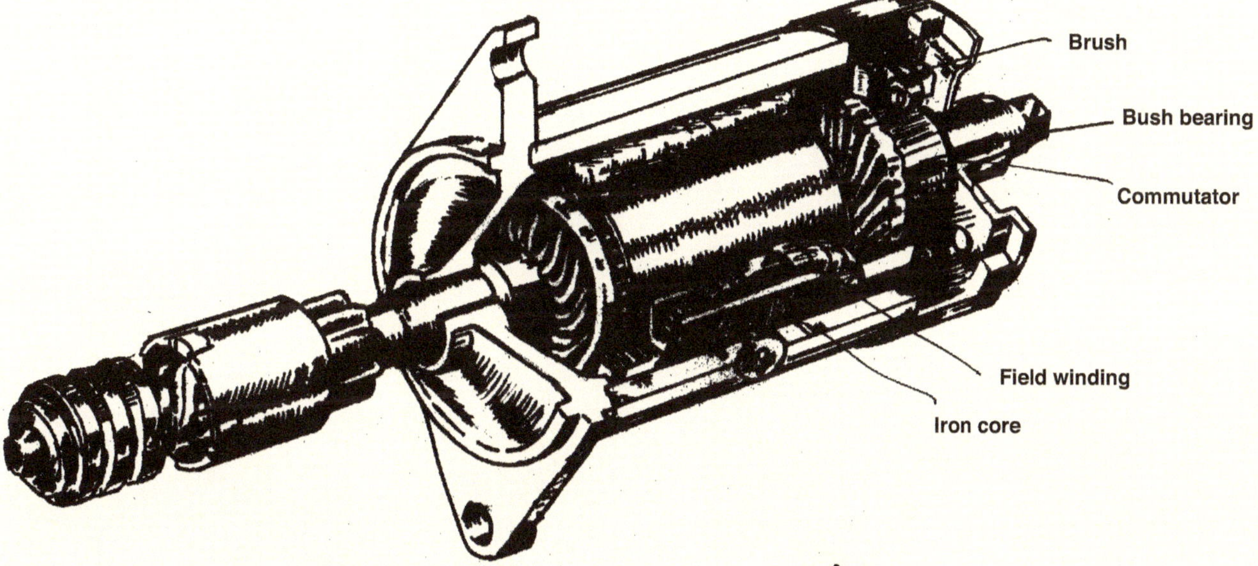

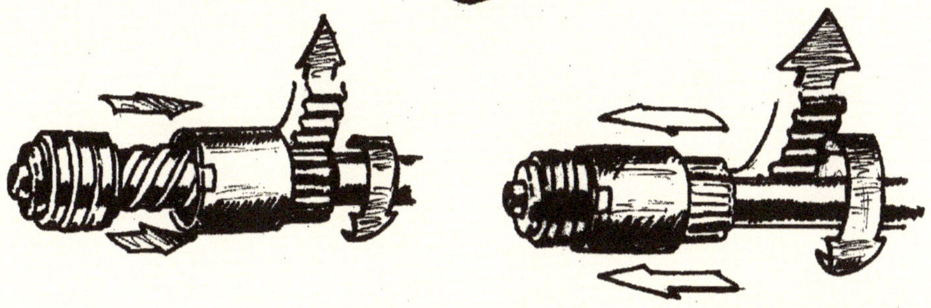

Pinion at starting position.

Pinion moves out of mesh when engine fires.

ENTHUSIAST'S RESTORATION MANUAL SERIES

earth return strap may be heavier, but is more often steel and not generally insulated. Both of these conductors are important elements in the starter system and need to be checked before looking to the actual starter motor in the event of problems.

The motor is usually of the series variety, which is to say that both the field coils and rotating arm armature coils are supplied one after the other from a common source. This arrangement offers greater starting torque over the alternative 'shunt motor' in which the field and armature are supplied in parallel.

In operation, the starter motor is very reliable, though the carbon brushes are prone to wearing and so need regular replacement. Likewise, the commutator can become clogged with dust from the brushes, so a clean will never go amiss.

The solenoid is a remotely controlled switch used to energise the starter motor, power to control the solenoid comes from the key switch. On earlier vehicles that feature an inertia type starter, the job of the solenoid is primarily to avoid having to run heavy and high-powered cable up to the dashboard.

Vehicles fitted with pre-engaged starters use the magnetic plunger of the solenoid to actively push and pull the starter pinion in and out of mesh with the flywheel. This has the advantage of placing the gear in contact with the ring-gear before the motor is turning, thus reducing wear and the risk of sticking.

The solenoid is a very reliable piece of kit and not generally serviceable by the motorist. Separate solenoids are cheap and easily replaced.

3. THE IGNITION SYSTEM

The job of the ignition system is to produce a spark with which to ignite our fuel/air mixture, and to deliver this spark at the correct time; this is asking quite a lot given that a simple four-pot engine can run at up to 6000 revs per minute, and four cylinders times 6000 divided by two (4-stroke cycle) means that your ignition might have to issue two-hundred sparks per second. And each at the optimum time to detonate the charge.

To cope with the extra demands of more cylinders, many V8 engines will utilise two contact-breakers within one distributor. It is not unheard of for supercars to run a separate distributor for each bank of cylinders. Twin sparkplug systems have also been employed to improve the efficiency of the burn.

In order to produce a spark we need to boost our meagre 12 volts, or the current will not have sufficient 'pressure' to jump the sparkplug gaps. The HT or high tension (high voltage) is generated within the ignition coil and is controlled by opening and closing of the contact-breaker, which is housed within the distributor. The contact-breaker is opened by means of a rotating cam.

Many vehicles based on a 12V system will run the coil from

Solenoid shows terminals for battery cable plus central switching terminal and permanent live take-off on right (battery) side.

only 6 volts under normal conditions – during start-up the full battery voltage is used, but as the demands of the starter are so high this may be somewhat reduced. In order to drop the coil voltage to 6 volts, a ballast resistor is put in line, which is bypassed, during start-up.

To deliver the HT, the distributor also has a rotor, which contacts with the leads of the individual sparkplugs in their respective firing order. Standard firing order for a four-cylinder engine is usually 1, 3, 4, 2 but can be 1, 2, 4, 3 – number 1 cylinder is usually taken to be the one nearest to the radiator. A normal firing order for a V8 engine would be 1, 2, 7, 8, 4, 5, 6, 3 – number one being right front. Simply crossing any two plug leads would result in poor running – so check your particular engine spec.

The rotor-arm and contact-breaker are actuated by means of the engine's rotation, and will therefore be synchronised to it. We can utilise this property by means of a timing mark on the crank pulley.

A single revolution of the engine takes place within a fraction

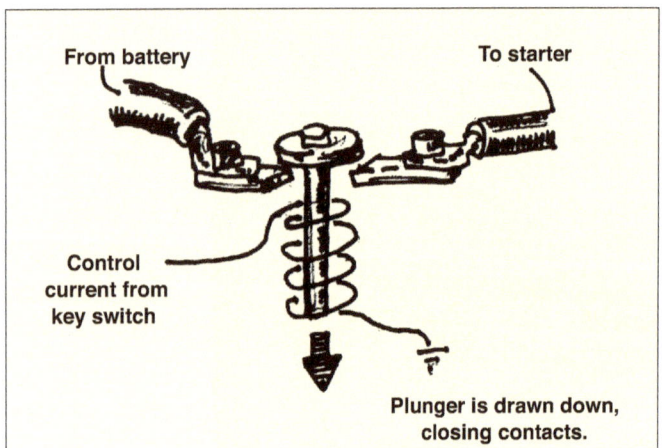

Principle of starter solenoid.

Centrifugal weights used to advance ignition timing.

THE FIVE SYSTEMS

of a second. The actual amount of time needed to burn our fuel/air mixture remains constant, so as engine speeds increase, the optimum time to deliver the spark will alter. To account for this, two methods of 'ignition advance' are commonly employed: centrifugal and vacuum advance.

Centrifugal advance. This method of ignition advancement is based upon a pair of weights, which rotate with the distributor shaft and act against a spring. As the engine speed increases, so the weights will tend to move outward, they are linked in such a way as to move the contact-breaker forward, in relation to the actuating cam on the shaft.

Vacuum advance. This method of advancement relies on the changes in inlet manifold pressure with increased engine load. A fine tube is taken from the manifold and linked to the distributor, under load the depression pulls against a diaphragm. This in turn is linked to the base plate onto which the contact-breaker is mounted. The net result is that suction from the manifold is used to move the contact-breaker relative to its actuating cam in such a way as to advance the ignition timing.

It is fairly standard practice to employ both types of advance on an engine, this is due to their different characteristics. The centrifugal system is better suited to accounting for changes in engine speed, while the vacuum is more adept when it comes to changes in load.

Proper maintenance of the ignition system is the key to successfully running a classic car. A full description of the ignition system and its components is given in the relevant section along with a complete set of diagnostic tests.

4. THE LIGHTING SYSTEM

The lighting system provides illumination to allow you to see and be seen. After the starter motor, the headlamps are the biggest draw on the power supply. Unlike the starter, the headlamps may be in use for many hours at a time. Sidelamps, though far smaller and primarily intended to allow other to see you, are also used for long periods.

As with all electric lighting the lamps rely on the heating effect, and will always be a compromise between brightness and longevity. Ageing wires can be a problem with older vehicles, but by far the biggest problem we will encounter when dealing with classic car lighting systems is corrosion.

Water ingress will lead to furred connections and so to poor current flow. Earth points in particular suffer from rust and any connections which feature differing metals such as steel, brass, or copper in close proximity, will promote bimetallic corrosion.

When investigating wiring, you may detect a voltage, but see no light at the relevant bulb. In such cases there is power, but not enough. Time spent cleaning connections will be worthwhile.

Caution – When altering or upgrading your vehicle's lighting system, you will need to be aware of the legal obligations that apply to your locality and particular application. Contact your local vehicles inspectorate or licensing office. Libraries or owner clubs are also worth consulting.

Morgan 3-wheeler headlamp.

Complete loom from 1950s saloon.

ENTHUSIAST'S RESTORATION MANUAL SERIES

5. ACCESSORIES, ANCILLARIES, OR AUXILIARIES

When talking about 'accessories' in the context of classic car electrics, we are usually referring to non-essential equipment such as the horn, radio or heated rear window. Exactly what we man by 'non-essential' is a tad contentious: the horn is a legal requirement and most of us would now regard a heated rear screen or heater fan as essential to safe driving. Not that long ago though, a heater was an optional extra, and many of us will remember being able to buy a heated screen that had to be glued in place.

Electric windows and powered convertible roofs are relatively recent to the British market, though such things will be found on many classic American automobiles. We will look at a range of items and most readers will find enough info to keep things working. We will also look at the option of fitting a radio and a few other goodies.

Sounds of the sixties ... and it still plays Tony Blackburn!

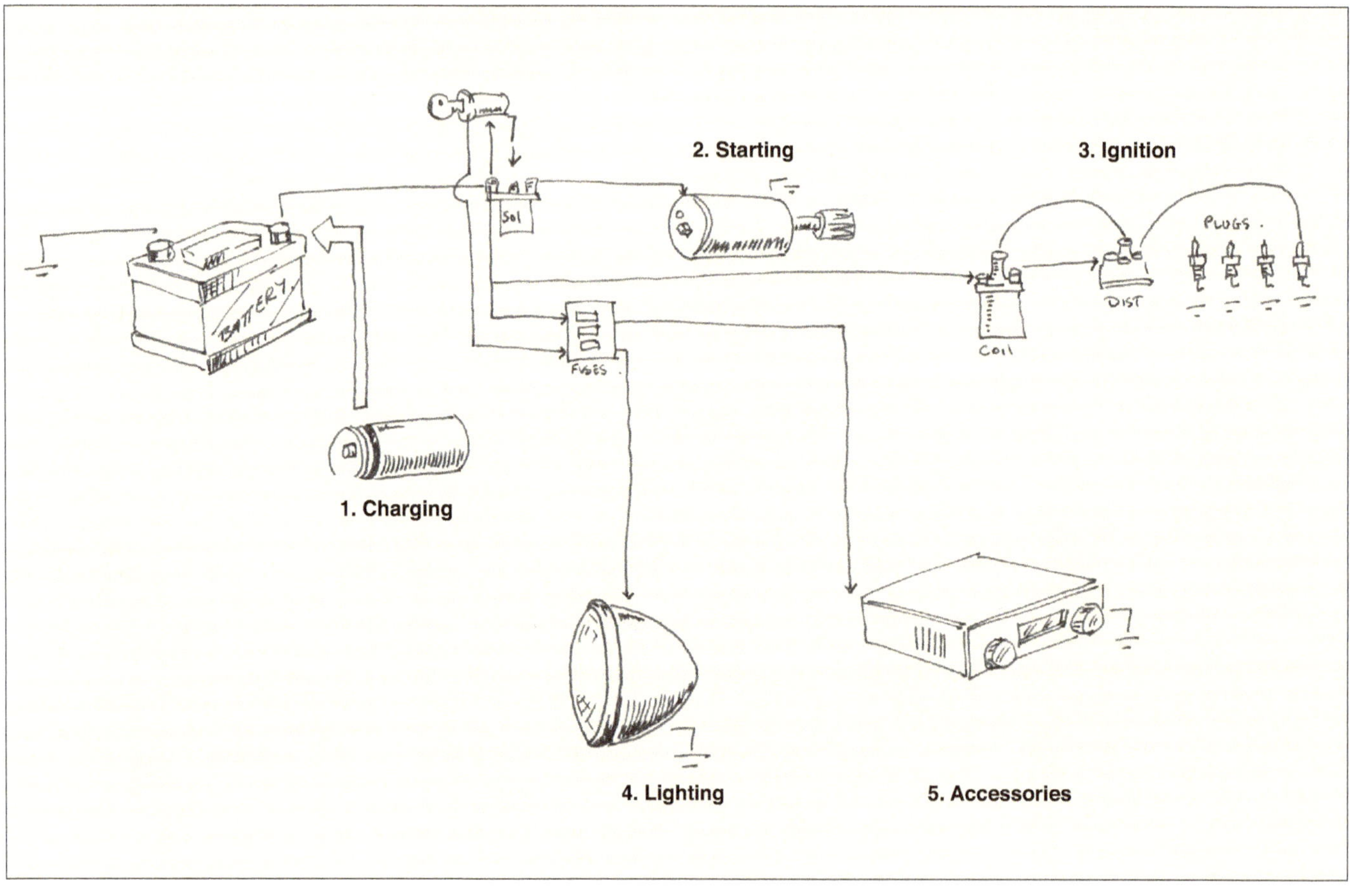

The five systems in sequence.

30

Chapter 8
The battery

The battery is the heart of your electrical system, it is your vehicle's reservoir of electrical power, and also the buffer which protects your system from surges and fluctuations in current and voltage. You should never attempt to run a motor vehicle without a suitable battery being in circuit.

As a rule whatever electrical problems you may encounter, the battery and its connections should be first on your list of checks. This is true even if the battery is brand-new and apparently in perfect working order.

The battery should be kept clean and must be well secured, both to its own mounting and at its terminals.

HOW A BATTERY WORKS

If you were to take a common lemon, and insert a piece of copper and a piece of zinc, an electrical potential would be present between the two metal 'electrodes'.

The acid, which we all know to be present in the lemon, would therefore be acting as an 'electrolyte'. That is to say, negative particles would tend to congregate around one electrode, while positive particles would gather at the other. If we were now to connect a meter across the two electrodes, we could measure a voltage and amperage. You can actually spin up a small motor from the lemon, which is always a good laugh. The lemon could therefore be regarded as a 'battery', or more correctly as a 'cell'; a group of lemons wired together would more properly be termed 'a battery'!

The lead-acid battery

The lead-acid battery, with which we are familiar, has been around since the earliest days of motoring and it is only now, a hundred years or so later, that any credible alternative has been seen.

Nickel-iron alkaline batteries offer superior performance to the lead-acid cell, but at a price. I feel it unlikely that many of us in the classic fraternity will go down this route just yet.

Cells

In a similar way to our lemon, the 12V lead acid battery is made up of a collection of cells each producing about 2V. Within each cell is a collection of lead plates which

A simplified cell.

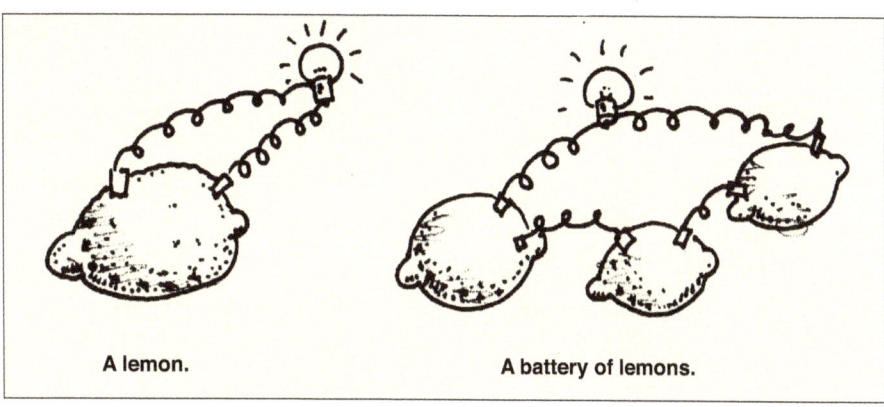

A lemon.   **A battery of lemons.**

ENTHUSIAST'S RESTORATION MANUAL SERIES

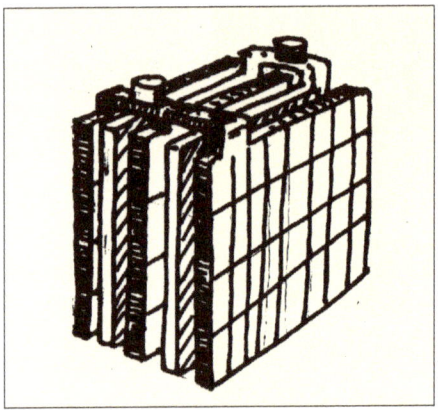

A battery cell.

are held in close proximity to each other. Between the plates is a solution of dilute sulphuric acid which acts as the electrolyte. To ensure that the negative and positive plates do not touch, they are separated by thin sheets of either glass-fibre or paper. This separating material is porous so as to allow free contact between the acid and the plates.

Voltage

In a battery of this type, the voltage is governed by the amount of cells. The individual cells are joined in series by lead contact strips. If there is a breach between the cells then the overall voltage of the battery will be greatly lowered. A 6V unit will contain three 2V cells and a 12V unit will contain six. A vehicle which employs a 24V system will usually use two 12V batteries in series. Many readers will be familiar with the early 12V MGBs which featured two 6V batteries under the rear seat.

Capacity

Overall capacity is governed by the surface area and number of plates. A larger battery will potentially contain a larger reserve of power and will generally be better suited to the heavier vehicle.

Manufactures have used three standards to denote a battery's capacity:

1. AH amp hours
2. Reserve capacity
3. Cold cranking

Amp hour rating is the most common rating and gives an idea of the total charge on offer, but it is a tad misleading. A battery rated at 40AH, might realistically deliver 2 amps for 20 hours, or 1 amp for 40 hours – but could it deliver 40 amps for 1 hour? Probably not. Needless to say a higher AH rating means more amps in store, but exactly how many?

Reserve capacity is the length of

A good battery installation is clean and secure. Failure here will undermine any other work.

The battery label shows capacity and give warnings.

time that a particular unit can deliver 25 amps at 25°C before the voltage drops to below 10.5V. If you can find this statistic, it is a realistic measure of performance for comparison.

Cold cranking or cold-discharge rate. This is a realistic measure of a battery's ability to get you going when you need it most. Unfortunately, American, British, and German ratings are all different. Have a chat with your supplier.

Battery casing

The box in which we place our lead plates

THE BATTERY

and sulphuric acid obviously needs to be strong, light, and resistant to chemical attack. Older battery casings tend to be made of a hard rubber, while modern batteries are generally manufactured from polypropylene plastic. This material is lighter and will tend not to breakdown with age.

The moulded casing is made in such a way as to isolate the cells and to hold the plates off the bottom, this is to avoid any sediment which might lead to a short between plates.

Most current batteries feature vent holes to allow any gases to be safely expelled, especially when charging. The exception to this rule is the 'sealed for life' type battery, which contains calcium. This type of battery is not well suited to the older car as the likelihood of 'gassing' is higher, if the charging voltage is not controlled to a very high degree.

Battery life

When it comes to buying car batteries, you will generally get what you pay for. Budget units with a guarantee of one year may well last only one year! But that is not to say that you shouldn't shop around, and the life of your battery can be maximised with a little care and regular maintenance.

BATTERY MAINTENANCE
External

It is essential that your battery be kept clean, as even a thin film of dirt may drain its power by leaching current across the terminals. Furred, dirty, or poorly fitted terminals will not conduct current well, which can lead to an under-charged battery. At worst, the terminals may overheat which could ignite any nearby grease.

A battery which is not properly secured to its mounting will rock or slide about, and such movement can cause fracturing or loosening of the terminal connections.

Terminals should be cleaned with a wire brush if they are seen to be furred or dirty. After the cables are refitted, they should be smeared with petroleum jelly or a similar product.

Check the condition of the cables and pay special attention to the earth point where the braided earth-strap meets the bodywork – this is a common point of corrosion and, therefore, resistance.

When replacing earth straps always fit the heaviest cable available – too light a wire will tend to get hot and eventually brittle.

Remember to check any cable between engine and body, as this does some of the work of the battery/bodywork earth strap.

Any spillage of acid must be cleaned up quickly as this will damage your paint work and encourage corrosion. Special acid-neutralising mats are available.

Continued spillage of acid may be a sign of over-charging, or a faulty battery, and should be investigated.

Keeping your battery clean will help keep it working – dirt can leach away charge across terminals.

Internal

Conventional (or older) batteries should be topped-up with distilled water every one thousand miles or as required. Low maintenance batteries need topping up approximately once a year. Maintenance-

Top up with distilled water; tap water will lead to premature calcification and failure.

ENTHUSIAST'S RESTORATION MANUAL SERIES

Charging. This old charger unit has a meter; newer models will probably have an LED display. Fast charging will reduce battery life, so buy a low-powered charger.

intend to lay-up your vehicle for a long period, it is advisable to disconnect or remove the battery and keep it in a state of at least 70 per cent charge.

As rule you should top-up the charge every month or so. The easiest way to do this would be to take the car for a spin, but as that is not always practical, you might consider a trickle charger which can be used to slow-charge the battery. In general it is not a good idea to 'fast-charge', except when totally neccessary (i.e. to get you home). Maintenance-free batteries in particular are not designed for fast charging.

The ideal charging rate for any particular unit can be determined from the spec on its label. A battery can be safely charged at a rate equivalent to $1/10$th of its amp hour rating for 10 hours or less until its voltage reaches 14.4 volts. An even safer bet would be to charge at $1/40$th of the amp hour rate for 50 hours. This assumes the battery to have been completely flat before charging. A battery which has been left totally flat for any time, may, in fact, be unable to take a full charge or it may appear to function but not for long – this is due to a build-up of sulphate on the plates which might be reversed with very gentle charging.

When charging any battery, observe the safety advice supplied with your charger and avoid sources of ignition including sparks. Any fumes given off during the charging process are toxic and potentially explosive.

The correct method of charging a battery is by running the vehicle to which it is fitted!

See below for the full lowdown on testing, charging, and the relevant science.

free batteries should not require topping up and are not designed to be opened; this type of unit is only suitable for vehicles fitted with an AC alternator charging system, as anything over 14.5V will cause gassing, leading to a loss of electrolyte.

It is often tempting to top-up a battery with tap water, and this will work for a while. However, tap water usually contains too much calcium and will lead to calcification of the plates and a shortened battery life.

When topping up your battery, do not overfill the cells as this will tend to dilute the acid unduly and may breach the partitions between the individual cells. As a rule you should fill the cells so that the plates are just submerged.

CHARGING

To get the best from your battery it is necessary to keep it charged, repeated or prolonged discharge will shorten its working life. If you

JUMP-STARTING OR BOOSTER-STARTING

We've all done it, and we all need to know how best to do it, without the risk of damage to car or person. Firstly you should get hold of the best quality leads you can – this need not mean that you have to spend big dosh on a fancy set, rather get a set that features a heavy gauge of (preferably) copper cable and good clips. Ideally these cables would also have an anti-surge device fitted but this is more important when starting newer machines with electronic circuits on board. Vehicles fitted with an alternator might sustain damage to the voltage regulator if a surge protector is not employed. Personally, I would recommend that you purchase one of the type used while Mig-welding.

Jump-start procedure

Make certain that the vehicle will not move if started – check brakes, chocks, and gearshift, etc. Place the live lead between the live (+) terminal of the dead battery and the live (+) terminal of the vehicle to be started. Be sure that the cables are connected correctly and will not foul any moving parts when the engine fires. Connect the earth lead between the earth (-) terminal of the dead battery and either the neg (-) terminal of the car to be started, or a suitable earth point in the engine bay. This latter method should ensure that the current gets to the starter, where we want it, rather than going to charge the battery. A suitable point would be the alternator bracket or similar. Be certain not to touch any live point and again watch out for anything that might foul when moving.

You may wish to leave the engine of the slave vehicle ticking over for a few minutes before attempting to start a car that is totally 'flat'. Do not rev the engine as the lack of battery resistance means that the flat car has no surge protection.

When cranking, check for any heating of the terminals, as this would indicate a poor contact. In emergencies, it is not unheard of for a person to squeeze the clips in order to get a vehicle going.

When the 'flat' car is running under its own steam, you may again wish to leave the two vehicles joined for a few minutes until warm. This will lessen the risk of repeated connection and disconnection due to stalling.

Always disconnect the earth (-) lead first, taking care not to

Jump starting is only for when really necessary. Run cables from battery to battery, or run the earth lead to a suitable earth on the slave car – this ensures the power runs through the starter motor as opposed to the flat battery.

THE BATTERY

allow anything to pass near moving or live parts. If you find yourself holding a pair of leads which are connected at one end to a live battery, be careful not to let them touch as this will result in violent sparking and possible damage to the battery, vehicle, or cables. Or in fact anything else nearby.

Jump-starting with two batteries

In extreme cases it is possible to employ two batteries to start a reluctant motor.

A. Two batteries in parallel will produce 12V at a higher amperage and may get things going. This is a pretty safe procedure.

B. Two batteries in series will produce 24V and will cause the starter to turn at a faster speed which may in turn draw a better fuel/air mixture and promote ignition.

As a 12V system is not designed to handle 24V it is obvious that this situation cannot be sustained for long. For one thing your starter motor is not meant to cope with the heat load, also your battery will not appreciate the higher charge rate. It works, but I cannot recommend it!

Jump-starter packs

In recent years a flood of jump-start power-packs have appeared on the market. These clever devices are gel-filled batteries and can, in some cases, jump-start several dozen flat cars from a single charge – or so they claim.

In truth the better units are everything they purport to be, but the cheaper ones are not quite. Personally, I think this is a brilliant advance and, if you can afford one, you can save yourself a lot of worry. Many models will have built-in lamps and compressors etc, and that is all fine, but remember that these 'extras' use power at the expense of the starting function.

BATTERY HANDLING AND SAFETY

Always handle a battery with respect and be ready to take action in the event of mishap.

Remember:

1. Batteries are heavy and often sited in awkward locations. Care must be taken when lifting a battery, so as not to cause spillage, sparking or damage to the person lifting. It is a good idea to invest in a proper lifting tool, and always wear eye protection and suitable gloves. Never attempt to move a battery in a car in which the engine is running.

2. Batteries are filled with acid. This is, in fact, dilute sulphuric acid and is able to 'eat' a variety of materials. Acid on the skin or in the eyes is a serious matter and after washing with copious amounts of clean water, medical attention should be sought.

If you keep an eye-wash in your workshop, you should check the label before using it to douse after an acid incident.

Acid spillages must be cleaned up promptly with clean water. Contaminated clothing should be removed and discarded after the acid has been doused. Heavy chemical-resistant gloves are useful for this job. See below for filling instructions.

3. Batteries are a store of electrical energy. Great care must be taken so as not to 'short' the battery, as this may

Jump-start pack. This little beauty has given years of sterling service. Keeping one of these in your car will make you a hero at club events!

A battery carrier is a safer option to lifting by hand.

35

ENTHUSIAST'S RESTORATION MANUAL SERIES

cause a fire or, worse, detonate any gasses produced by charging. Always disconnect the earth (-) terminal first and avoid contacting any conductor to the live terminal.

4. Batteries have been known to explode. The process of charging will often produce hydrogen gas which is highly explosive, and must not be allowed to build up.

Always ensure proper ventilation and avoid any sources of ignition- including the charger itself.

Remember to connect the neg- last and disconnect it first.

5. Battery fumes are toxic. Any sulphurous 'rotten egg' smell, while charging or driving is a sign of too high a voltage or a failing unit.

6. Battery filling. Some batteries are supplied 'dry', this allows for safer and easier storage and avoids any issue of shelf-life. In such a case you will be required to mix the solution of acid and water before filling the case. Instructions will be supplied and you will need a heavy acid resistant apron and gloves, along with eye protection and some substantial glass vessels to mix in. The rule is always mix the acid to the water, and never the other way around – personally, I wouldn't do this if you paid me, its not worth the hassle!

Battery testing and the science bit

We have two approaches to testing the condition of a lead acid battery:

Firstly, we can measure the output under different conditions.

Secondly, we can measure the electrolyte.

Heavy discharge tester.

Proprietary battery/starting tester. It does exactly what it says on the label!

Heavy discharge test

The heavy discharge tester is basically a pair of handles and probes with a large low-resistance conductor fixed between them. A volt-meter id fitted across this crude circuit. If we force the probes against the terminals of our battery, we can measure the voltage as it drops under the load of discharging. The meter will indicate ranges for 'good' and 'bad' for a given time span. Any 'gassing' will reveal a faulty cell.

The downside of this simple test is that it may exacerbate an existing problem, and repeated use of the heavy discharge tester will quickly flatten your battery.

Simple volt-meter readings

A reading across the terminals of your battery should give some idea of its state of health. We understand our system to work at 12 volts but it is normal for an alternator to put out something nearer to 14V. Likewise many chargers will produce a similar value. With this in mind it is a good idea to wait a few minutes after charging before measuring a batteries voltage.

*A volt-meter reading of between 13.2V and 12.6V indicates a battery which is fully charged.

*A reading of 12.2V suggests that your battery is in need of a charge.

THE BATTERY

The hydrometer (shown with packaging) is really just a pipette with a float in it. It provides a quick method of checking electrolyte condition.

*A reading of 11V shows a battery in serious need of a charge, continued drain from a battery in this state of charge may result in permanent damage.

Hydrometer test
The hydrometer is essentially a 'pipette' with a float inside it. As our battery discharges, so the electrolyte changes from dilute sulphuric acid to water. This partly explains why we top-up with water and not acid. Anyhow, as the electrolyte changes so does its relative density, thus the float will sit at a different level depending on our battery's state of charge.

The hydrometer will have a scale indicating the percentage of charge, this is usually colour coded. It can be used in conjunction with a battery charger to ensure optimum charging.

Mini-hydrometers are available and cost very little.

The science in a nutshell
Many chemical changes occur within the battery cell during the charge/discharge cycle.

Discharge
If our cell is fully charged, the positive plates are made of lead peroxide, while the negative plates are made of 'spongy' lead. At this point the electrolyte consists of dilute sulphuric acid with a specific density of 1.270 to 1.290 (compared with water). During use (discharge) the sulphur in the acid combines with the plates and forms lead sulphate, and both hydrogen and oxygen are released during this process, these will combine to form water and further dilute the electrolyte.

As the cell discharges further, the plates both turn to lead sulphate which is bulkier than either lead peroxide or spongy lead. This difference in size results in some distortion of the plates if discharging occurs too rapidly. This can result in some of chemical paste breaking away from the plate and premature failure of the cell.

At 70 per cent of charge the electrolyte has a density of 1.230 to 1.250.

In a state of half charge the electrolyte has a density of 1.200.

A discharged or flat battery has an electrolyte density of 1.110 to 1.130.

Charging
In order to recharge the cell, a current must be forced through it. The charging voltage must be higher than the cells own voltage. This is why we use a charging voltage of about 14V from the generator to charge a 12V unit. Remember that the voltage is divided between the cells –14V by 6 cells = 2.3 'ish' volts per cell.

During the recharging process, lead peroxide reforms on the positive plate using oxygen from the electrolyte, while Sulphur is released from both sets of plates which strengthens the acid. The other result of the changes is that the negative plate returns to being spongy lead.

www.velocebooks.com/www.veloce.co.uk
All books in print • New books • Special offers • Gift Vouchers

Chapter 9
Generator 1 – the DC dynamo

The direct current generator is usually referred to as a 'dynamo'. This type of device was fitted to the majority of vehicles manufactured between the 1930s and the mid-1970s, many of which would have featured positive earth wiring. In keeping with this, assume everything in this section to be of that polarity.

The dynamo relies on a simple principle but is of complex construction; typically it will feature twenty-eight separate coil-windings in the central moving rotor or armature. These are the generating coils and feed DC current through a pair of carbon brushes and a 'commutator'. The segments of the commutator relate to the individual coils.

The field coils are held within the body of the unit and use a soft iron casting to concentrate their magnetic effect.

Due to its construction, the dynamo is limited in top speed to about 6000rpm, beyond which it may overheat. As such, vehicles with a top engine speed of 6000rpm – which accounts for the majority of our domestic classics! – will usually have the dynamo turned by a pulley which rotates at the same rate as the crank pulley that powers it.

Unfortunately, this means that at lower engine speeds the device is not turned fast enough to generate any power, and if not properly regulated will drain electricity from the battery.

DYNAMO MAINTENANCE

Considering its complexity the dynamo is a very reliable piece of kit. Like anything, though, it does require some maintenance from time to time.

Bearings

Models from the fifties and before will probably have been originally fitted with porous bronze bearings, these require oiling on a regular basis. Many models may feature oiling holes near the commutator behind which is a felt washer which acts as a reservoir of lubricant. Other features you may find are the removable bearing cup, and the lubricating plug.

Worn bushes and bearings need replacing to avoid serious damage as the moving parts are in very close proximity to the stationary items.

An overly tightened fan belt will lead to premature failure of the main bearing.

Carbon pick-up brushes and the segmented commutator are prone to wear, or fouling with dust.

Total dismantling of the average dynamo is not beyond the home mechanic. Typically the unit is held together by two long through-bolts, and these, as the name suggests, run the entire length of the device. To replace a main bearing, the rotor (armature) will have to be placed in a vice so that the pulley can be removed before the bearing is extracted. Careful use of a suitable drift will facilitate the fitting of the new bearing set.

Dynamo in situ. It pivots on its mount to adjust belt tension.

GENERATOR 1 – THE DC DYNAMO

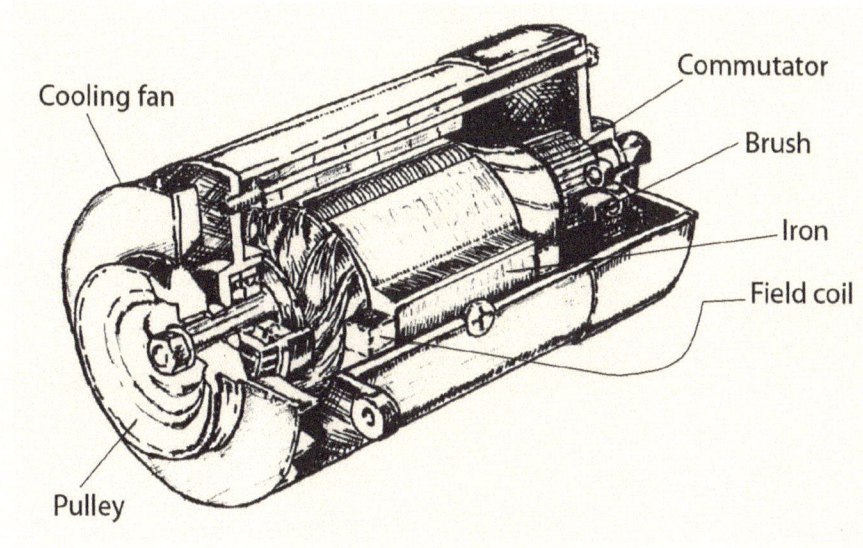

A simplified dynamo.

Rear of unit shows commutator, brush set and contacts.

The 1972 Beetle unit gives good access to the brush set while in situ.

Standard Lucas dynamo; this type of unit was to be found on millions of British cars.

Be certain to make note of the many spacers and washers which you will encounter in the average dynamo, and always use soft jaws if employing a vice.

Bronze bush type bearings are fairly soft and need a bit of care when being pushed into place; never strike them directly with a hammer, a wooden or copper drift is always better, and pushing is always preferable to hitting. Older porous bronze bushes will need to be soaked in a light oil for 24 hours prior to fitment. These have largely been replaced with items of a more modern bronze alloy.

Brushes & commutator

Brushes are easily replaced, and a lightly worn commutator can be cleaned with a little fine abrasive. It is not uncommon to find a removable plate or window through which the brushes can be accessed. The gaps between the commutator segments can be tidied up by 'undercutting' them with a piece of hacksaw blade, or by scraping with a pin. Use glass-paper as its grit is non-conducting and undercut by no more than 0.5-1mm.

A commutator which has worn due to an eccentric bearing may need turning on a lathe to correct, or you may find it simpler (in most cases) to replace the entire unit.

Cleaning

Traditional wisdom states that the commutator be cleaned with carbon tetrachloride. This is a highly toxic substance no longer sold over the counter.

The wires that make up the windings found within the dynamo are often insulated with lacquer. In view of this, it is not a good idea to try to clean any of the internals with an aggressive solvent as this may damage the lacquer and lead to a short circuit.

Some people have suggested using petrol for cleaning, but given the likelihood of sparks from the brushes, a flammable liquid is not a good thing to have around a working dynamo.

However, a clean cloth with a little fine solvent such as thinners, petrol, spirit-wipe, etc., can be used to wipe the commutator. Be sure to remove any excess and do not refit until dry.

TESTING
Windings

While it is possible to test the continuity of any of the coils, it is beyond the scope of the home enthusiast to replace any of the windings. This work, if necessary, must be entrusted to an experienced professional.

Testing the dynamo output

Having checked the fan belt and all the relevant connections at the battery terminals and regulator etc., it might be a

ENTHUSIAST'S RESTORATION MANUAL SERIES

Commutator care

The commutator can be improved with glass paper.

Dust and oil can be removed with degreaser or petrol.

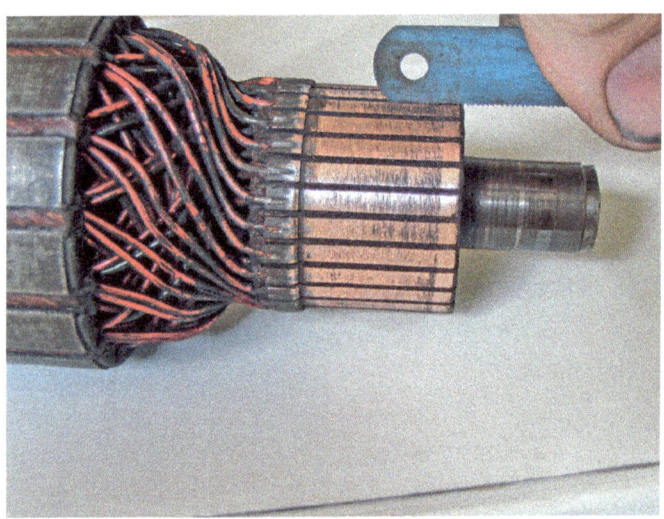

If worn, segments can be 'undercut' with a hacksaw blade.

Brush set and holders are in need of a good clean.

Check fan belt tension – this is normally +/½in (25mm) on the longest section of belt.

good idea to take a peek at the brushes and commutator (if this is possible in situ) – any sign of solder or spatter would mean that the unit is a gonner.

A lack of voltage at the battery would suggest that the generator is at fault. The steps are as follows, starting with the simplest:

1. Remove both wires from the dynamo (do not confuse them). Place a bridge of wire between the two terminals, and from the centre of this take a feed to a lamp and on to earth. Run the engine: if the lamp lights at tickover, raise the speed gently and the brightness should increase – this is normal.

2. To check the voltage you will require a meter set to 0-30V.

3. Remove both cables as before and place a bridge of wire across the two terminals. Now place the volt-meter between the bridge and a good earth – negative to the dynamo and positive to earth as this is a positive earth vehicle. Ensure that the lights etc. are off, and run the engine at about 1000rpm – the exact speed will vary from model to model but must be above the cutout speed of the system. A reading of about 15V is desirable, while a reading of 4-6V would sugges that the armature is faulty.

4. To test the continuity of the cables from the dynamo you could simply use

40

GENERATOR 1 – THE DC DYNAMO

Dismantling a dynamo

Remove through bolts – a squirt of oil may help as these can shear off.

Rear plate comes off.

Rear plate carries brush set and bronze bush.

Armature comes out. Look for signs of wear which suggest worn bearings.

Field coils and core magnets housed in casing. Again, look for wear.

Main bearing housing. Pulley must be removed to allow access.

Dirty commutator. Note position of any washers or shims.

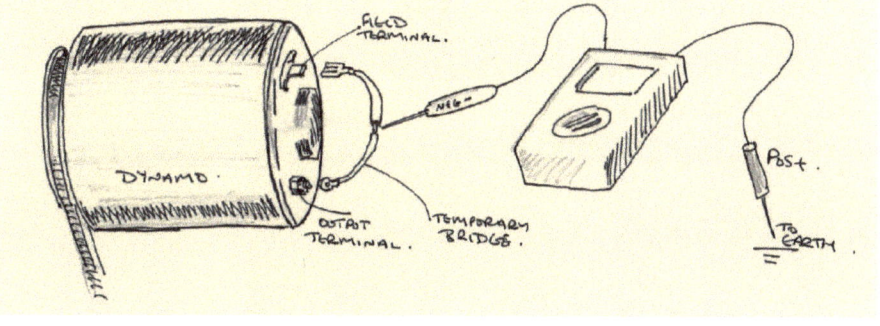
Field coils and core magnets housed in casing. Again, look for wear.

the resistance setting on the meter or, with the temporary bridge still in situ, disconnect one cable from the regulator box and install the volt-meter in line. A poor reading will show the cable to be faulty, while a good one would suggest the box is the problem. Repeat this test on the other cable – be careful to reconnect the cables D to D, and F to F, and remove the bridge.

5. Dynamo-amp test. Start by disconnecting the dynamo leads from the control box (terminal 'B' or 'A') and interposing a 40A ammeter, then close the regulator contacts with a clip (being careful not to short this to anything else.) Next, run the engine at about 4500rpm with a full load, i.e. lights etc. You should get reading near to the value stated on the unit. The dynamo should be able to produce its full output regardless of your battery's condition.

A fluctuating reading suggests dirty points in the regulator, while a steady but incorrect reading may be corrected by adjusting the points.

The voltage regulator/control box

A typical control box as found in millions of British and European classics is shown here. Similar items will be seen on most vehicles from the time period that we are concerned with.

The job of the control box/voltage regulator is to keep the voltage and current to within safe limits. It does this by supplying current to the field coils of the dynamo, thus governing the amount of current generated in the rotor.

By taking the dynamo out of circuit

ENTHUSIAST'S RESTORATION MANUAL SERIES

The Lucas two-bobbin regulator as found in many older cars.

This internal view of a regulator shows two bobbins.

Later units will have a terminal marked 'WL' – warning lamp, while earlier models will supply the tell-tale from a line which runs from the D terminal to the ignition switch.

Maintenance

In some cases maintenance will consist of little more than cleaning, or ensuring a good earth and connections.

Cleaning

To clean the internal contacts it is usual to insert a piece of abrasive paper and, while manually closing the points, draw the abrasive through the contacts. Conventional wisdom states that glass paper be used to clean the cutout, while the regulator is cleaned with emery paper, and never the other way around. Cleaning of the contacts is completed with a wipe of methylated spirit or similar, to remove any residue.

Try to ensure that the regulator box and its surround are kept clean and free of rust which could inhibit a sound earth.

Checking & adjustment

If your battery is being over-charged, then the problem is almost certain to lie within the regulator. You may wish to simply replace the unit or hand over any further testing to a specialist. But if you really want to carry on ...

The Lucas three-bobbin regulator was used in millions of cars ...

... this internal view shows adjusters.

at low revs, the control box prevents any back-flow of current. The exact minimum speed will depend on the age and type of vehicle in question, and should be checked prior to making any assumptions regarding the effectiveness of the charging system.

The other job of the unit is to prevent over-charging of the battery.

Inside the typical box you will see either two or three 'bobbins' that are essentially magnetic switches, these are shown arranged from left to right – voltage regulator, current regulator, and cutout.

A two box arrangement will consist of one current regulator and one cutout. The cutout has the job of switching the field coils on and off.

It is important to identify the contacts to the box before attempting any work, as failure to correctly connect the dynamo to the unit can result in serious damage.

So far as domestic vehicles are concerned most will be labelled 'E' – earth, 'F' – field, 'D' – dynamo main supply. The output will usually be either A/A1 or B/B1 – one of these will probably go to the battery while the other will feed the ignition switch or possibly run to the fuse board.

GENERATOR 1 – THE DC DYNAMO

The following is applicable only to adjustable units and often requires a special tool and a fairly robust ammeter (+/-40A). You will also need a thermometer and your volt-meter set to 0-20V.

You typically see a difference in switching voltage in the region of 1V between the ambient temperature of 10°C/50°F and 40°C/104°F, but you will again need the exact spec for your particular vehicle.

The test is not difficult, but must be performed quickly (30 seconds or so) to avoid possible error, as heating of the coils will invalidate the result.

Regulator check and adjust for a three-bobbin regulator

Having removed the cover and cleaned the contact points, place a piece of card between the cutout points to disable them. Connect the volt-meter between the contact D and a good earth point. Now run the engine up to between 2500 and 3000rpm and hold it steady. This will depend on the cutout spec of the car in question.

The voltage should settle to a steady value between 14.5V and 15.5V – dependent on model and temperature.

If the voltage continues to fluctuate then this would suggest dirty contacts, while a stable reading which was either high or low would suggest that the regulator needed adjusting.

If your reading shows that the voltage is continuing to rise with engine speed outside of the normal limits, then this would suggest that the control box is in need of replacement.

Regulator check and adjust for a two-bobbin regulator

The test is similar to the above but the A and A1 leads must be disconnected and joined together, the volt-meter is set between the D and a good earth in the same way as before.

The dynamo output test is detailed above with the other Dyno tests.

To check and re-set the cutout

Three-bobbin
Set a volt-meter between the 'WL' tab and a good earth point. Now start the engine and apply an electrical load, gradually up the revs and watch for the contacts to close – you would expect this to occur typically at between 12.7V and 13.3V. Any adjustments should be made in very small increments.

Two-bobbin
Again the test is much the same but the A and A1 leads must first be detached and joined. The meter is again set between the D and a sound earth.

The drop-in voltage can usually be adjusted by simply bending the contact and observing the result.

The above is generalised and based upon a variety of 50s and 60s British classics. You should have no trouble obtaining the complete specifications for your particular engine or vehicle. If in doubt, contact the relevant owners' club, or an auto-electrical specialist.

This VW regulator is a simple two-bobbin design.

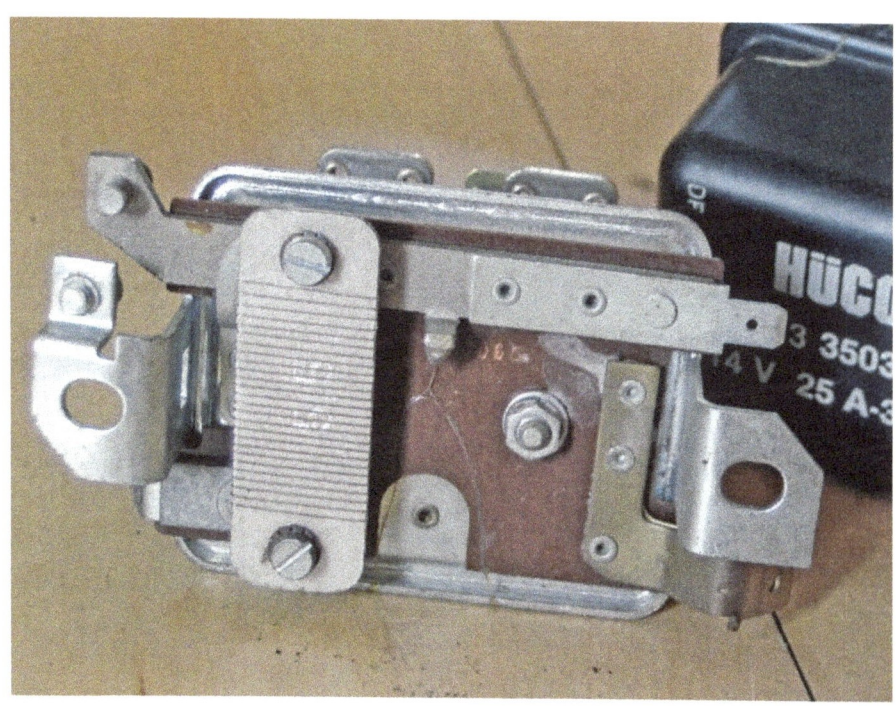

The rear view of the VW unit shows connections.

Chapter 10
Generator 2 – the AC alternator

A generator which produces an alternating current is referred to as an alternator for obvious reasons. All but the earliest alternators used in automotive applications are fitted with a built in 'rectifier', this converts the alternating AC output to a DC direct current', which can then be used by the battery.

Though the alternator and dynamo use the same principles to generate power, they are of quite different construction. Where the dynamo has its generating coils in the central moving rotor, the alternator shows the reverse. By building the generating field coils into the static body of the unit it is possible to run the alternator at higher speeds and produce greater volumes of electrical current, compared to the older DC unit. Accordingly, you will notice that a smaller pulley is used to drive the alternator, which turns at a higher speed relative to the engine crank. In turn, the alternator is more effective at slower engine speeds and can produce a reasonable charging current at tick-over.

Alternator construction

Most alternators will have three generator coils built into the body around a laminated soft iron 'stator'. The generating coils will be arranged in such a manner, that they will overlap each other, and will be configured as either a 'star' or 'delta' which is to say approximately in series or parallel. The star arrangement will tend to produce a higher voltage, while the delta will give a higher current. Most of us need not worry beyond this.

The 'armature' or rotor features only one coil, which is

Alternators in situ: over-restored or rather tatty?

GENERATOR 2 – THE AC ALTERNATOR

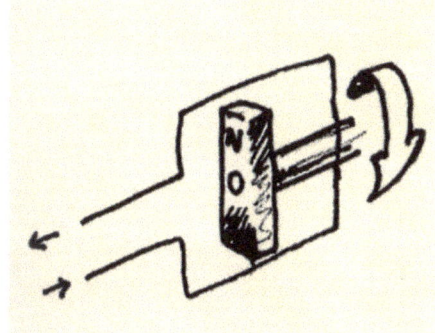

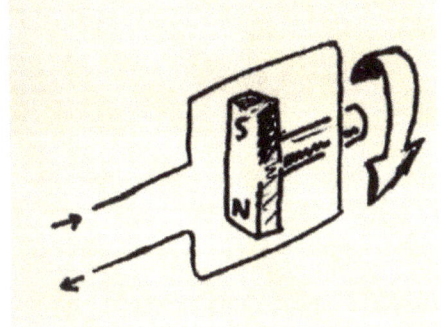

Principle of the alternator.

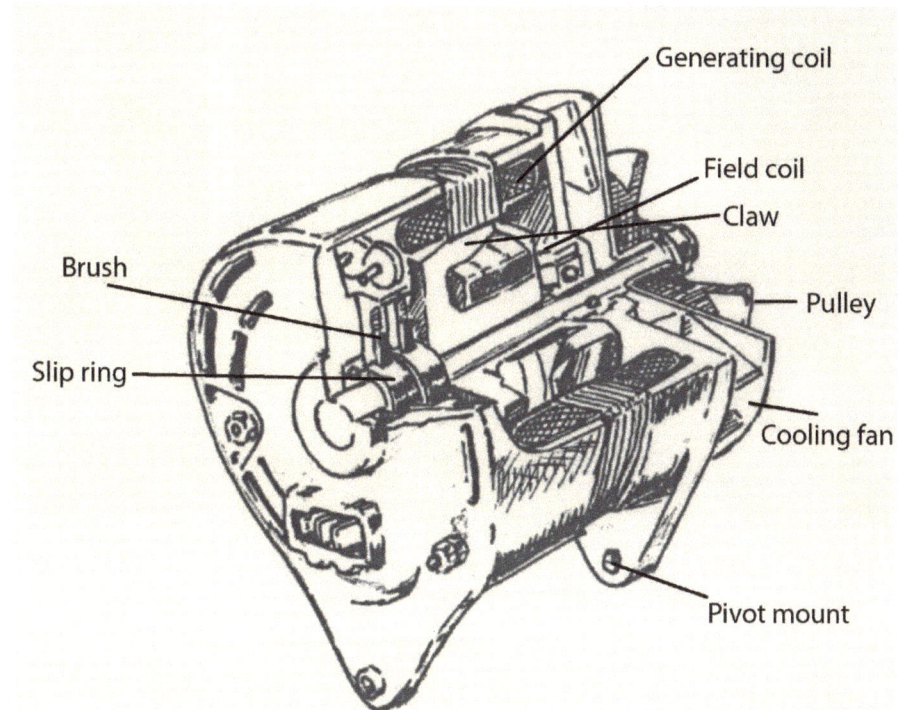

Alternator.

The armature shows slip-rings and claws.

Generator coils, brush set and diode pack. This unit is not designed to be user serviced.

This unit offers a removable 'brush-box' for inspection and replacement.

More typical connections: two are for output, the smaller is the tell-tale lamp.

Pivoting bracket and adjuster.

wrapped around a soft iron core. The ends of the armature core are extended and turned over the coil in the form if interlocking 'claws'. This arrangement is known as the 'claw-pole' rotor, and typically has either 12 or 16 claws, the polarity dependent on which end of the core they are connected to.

As the fingers are arranged alternately, so the current that is induced in each coil as they pass will tend to alternate correspondingly.

The 'field coil' of the armature is fed by a pair of 'slip-rings' and carbon brushes sited at the rear of the unit. Many models will allow for replacement of the brushes by means of a removable 'brush-box'.

ENTHUSIAST'S RESTORATION MANUAL SERIES

Fan belt pulleys and alternator adjustment strap: compare the relative size of the pulleys.

A 1957 Riley with AC conversion – practicality over originality.

Alternators which do not easily allow for brush replacement are generally not designed for user servicing.

Also at the rear of the unit will be a diode pack: this does the job of rectifying the output. The diode pack, although not the most complicated piece of electronics in the world, is not designed to be serviced.

The body of the stator is mounted into a cast metal casing – referred to as an end bracket, this will usually feature a pivot mounting. The mounting may include rubber bushing or spacers.

As you might imagine, laminated soft iron is prone to corrosion, and an alternator which has been left at the mercy of the elements will not generally fare well.

Alternator maintenance & servicing

As we have seen, we as home enthusiasts are limited in what we can do with an alternator in times of trouble – it behoves us to keep the things in good working order for as long as is possible.

Fan belt tension. Too high a tension of the fan-belt will lead to premature wearing of the bearings in your alternator, and, ultimately, to its failure. Too slack a belt will result in a hideous screaming as you turn on your headlamps or other electrical load.

Most European vehicles will feature a pivot or articulated mounting which will allow for adjustment of the pulley belt. Big American engines more often show a 'serpentine' belt which is more likely to have an idler or jockey wheel to provide the tension. This may be sprung or manually set. As a rule, a correctly set belt will allow no more than 1in of deflection on its longest stretch. That is to say plus and minus $1/2$in (+/-13mm) if pressed with a finger.

A belt which has been allowed to slip may become 'glazed' and cracked due to heating. Worn mountings will cause the belt to run out of line with the other pulleys and this will lead to vibration and premature wear. A good squirt of WD40 in and around your alternator won't go amiss, and a new belt with a major service, though not strictly necessary, is not really an extravagance!

Replacing a dynamo with an alternator

Though perhaps not true to the spirit of classic motoring, an alternator in place of the dynamo will provide a lot more power and the option for many more ancilliaries. Select a unit which matches the size of your engine, as well as the space in which it is to be fitted.

It is imperative that the belt runs true, so entrust bracket fabrication to someone experienced. Any mechanical failure here could prove costly or dangerous. It may be that a later version of your engine was fitted with an AC system, if so the parts you need could be available.

Control box and polarity change

If you wish to keep your vehicle as positive earth then a dual polarity alternator is an option, as is the simple route of tapping the output into the existing control box. The alternator will have its own regulator.

To convert your positive earth car to negative earth is actually quite simple.

Contrary to common belief (and common sense) reversing the polarity of the starter motor does not cause it to rotate in the other direction, and this is true of most of your vehicle's components. Electric fuel pumps may prove an exception but as most of them are isolated from the bodywork, it is simply a matter of swapping the wires to get things going.

Caution! – Radios can be damaged by reversing their polarity.

Chapter 11
The starter motor

STARTING THE ENGINE

In order to start the engine it must be rotated at about 50rpm (100rpm on more modern vehicles); at slower speeds it is unlikely that the carburettor would be able to draw a usable fuel/air mixture. In order to generate enough torque to turn the engine at this rate, a starter motor cranks the engine via a ring gear mounted around the flywheel; the ratio of pinion to flywheel is in the order of 10 to 1 and this increases the effective turning power to a usable degree.

A range of starter motor tests is detailed at the end of this section.

The inertia starter

The earlier inertia or 'Bendix' type, named after the company which first produced it, has the starting pinion mounted on its front end. When the motor is activated, the pinion is drawn toward the motor body along a helical spline, and into mesh with the ring gear. When the engine fires it rotates the pinion faster than the motor; as this happens the same spline will tend to pull the pinion out of mesh.

You will notice that the pinion has bevelled edges to its teeth, which allow for an easier mesh, but as the impact is fairly violent, after a while you can expect to see some deformation or burring of this area. The disadvantage of the inertia starter is that if the engine 'coughs' but fails to start, the pinion will not be in mesh to immediately restart it. This may lead to a lot of 'faffing about' as the engine coughs and splutters but doesn't actually start.

Another problem is that the pinion and its thread are exposed to dust from the clutch, if this mixes with any oil which might be present, then an unholy black porridge will form, which will cause the pinion to stick, leading to the situation mentioned previously.

Pinion stuck in mesh?

To free-up a stuck pinion on a manual vehicle, turn off the ignition, let off the handbrake, and set the car in gear, then 'shunt' the vehicle back and forth. Some models will feature a square peg protruding from the rear of the motor case – this is an extension of the armature and may be used to wiggle free the pinion.

Inspect brushes & commutator

The carbon brushes of the starter are designed to be replaced as their wear is an integral part of normal use. To this end, many starters will feature an access window or band. Removal of the cover band will allow the commutator and brushes to be inspected and cleaned. If you are to replace the brushes then a hook of wire can be inserted through the window and used to lift clear the brush springs.

The job of actually replacing the brushes demands removal of the motor from the car and removal of the end plate. After refitting the brushes, the same method can be employed to re-set the springs to their working position. See over.

Bendix inertia starter pinion in resting position ...

... and in starting position. Note helical spline.

ENTHUSIAST'S RESTORATION MANUAL SERIES

The starter motor is returned to its spiritual home - the kitchen table.

Cover-band removed to allow access: note terminal and end peg.

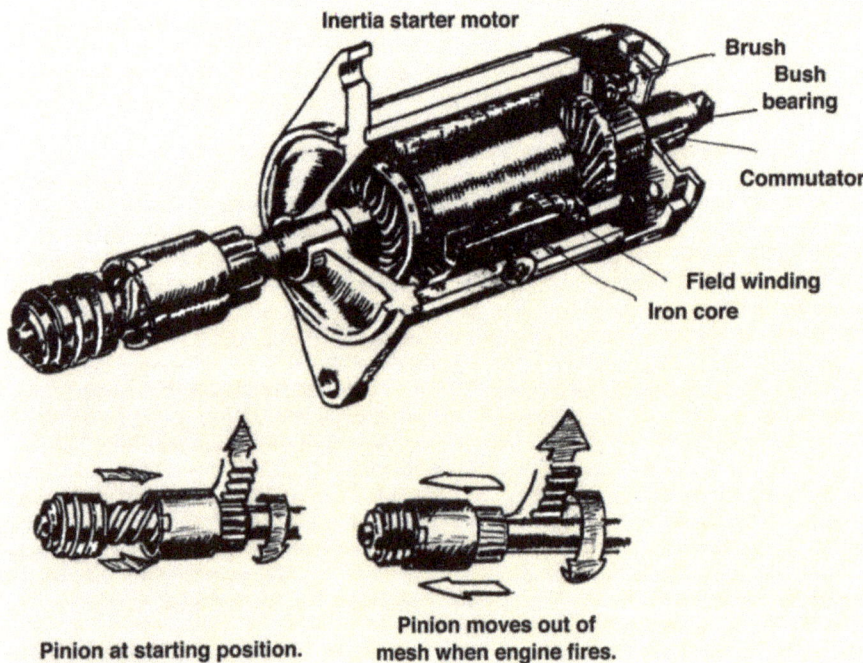

Pinion at starting position.

Pinion moves out of mesh when engine fires.

Removal

If the motor must be dismantled, then this will be a job within the reach of most home mechanics. The actual motor is typically fixed by only two bolts to the gear box, a third may also be found which could enter from behind. Another thing to look out for is a locating peg. A normal tool-kit should suffice, but be prepared to undo any fixings the hard way, by which I mean using a spanner, a fraction of a turn at a time. You may find you need to slacken exhaust pipes and the like to allow access.

Before removing the motor you must first ensure that the car is secure, then disconnect the battery, or risk a violent short. Next remove the cables at the starter end, and tidy these out of the way. If, having undone the mountings, the starter refuses to budge, a sharp tap from a copper mallet will usually work wonders. To extract the unit you may have to give it a bit of 'wiggle' – be careful, the thing is quite heavy!

Cleaning the pinion & commutator

When cleaning a starter pinion, you should use a paintbrush and petrol or other fine solvent – never use an oil, and never grease the pinion. At most a little pencil lead will do as a lubricant.

Petrol is also the chosen solvent for cleaning the commutator, but be certain not to let this get into the windings and thoroughly dry before use. A badly or eccentrically worn commutator might be corrected on a lathe.

A scruffy commutator can be tidied up with glass-paper in the same way as that

Solenoid with starter end cable.

Later models give access to the brush set and commutator via an end plate. Note the terminal.

48

THE STARTER MOTOR

Through bolts removed - these are tight and can shear off.

Tap with a mallet to loosen: note locating pips.

Withdraw armature from body.

Field coils and brush set retained within body.

Brushes are easily accessed through hole.

This commutator is badly worn but still works. Note position of washers or shims.

Clean commutator with contact cleaner or spirit-wipe, abrade with glass-paper, but never undercut segments (see dynamo).

Pinion may also show wear – this could cause sticking.

Clean pinion with petrol or degreaser and dry well.

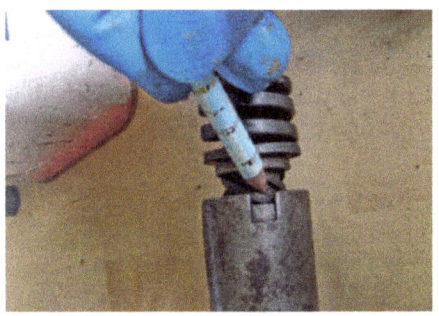
Never oil the pinion, at most use pencil lead to lubricate.

Wire hook used to lift brush and spring. An old brake spring is ideal.

Pay attention to terminal post - spacers and insulators must be clean and sound.

ENTHUSIAST'S RESTORATION MANUAL SERIES

from a dynamo, but in this case you do not undercut the gap between the segments.

Fitting new brushes
As mentioned above, many motors will have a cover band or access window through which the brushes can be inspected. It is useful to utilise this window to unhook the brush springs and set them to one side. After cleaning, or replacement of the brushes, the same access point can be used to place the springs back in working position.

Dismantling the motor
The typical motor is held together with two 'through bolts' with nuts on their back end. When undone, these will allow for dismantling from the rear to the front. The pinion and front plate do not usually need removal for routine maintenance.

To replace the carbon brushes you should hook the springs out of the way and carefully withdraw the soft carbon contact. The pig-tail wires from the brushes are soldered and will need to be cut if the brushes are to be replaced. Minimum brush length is in the region of 1/3in (8mm). If the brushes are of the correct length, but are sticking, you may polish them with a fine file or similar.

New brushes
New brushes must be properly soldered to the contacts or the motor will not operate satisfactorily. As the same current which supplies the field windings is also used to feed the armature, you can expect to find two pig-tail wires on each brush.

The brush holders and rear bush are commonly found mounted on the rear plate of the motor. If no access window is provided, then you should lift the brush springs clear of the brushes and set them in on the brush holders until the commutator has been re-fitted. After replacing the end plate you should be able to set the springs into their working position (on the brushes) using a fine screwdriver from behind the end plate.

Your starter may have two or four brushes, these will work in pairs, with one pair possibly wired to each other.

Bushes
The bearings will usually be of the bush type, the rear one is an easy job to replace: an appropriate threaded 'tap' can be used to withdraw the old bush, and a suitable drift employed to push the new one home.

The front bush bearing is a more involved job because it requires the removal of the pinion set. Original porous bronze bushes will require soaking in light oil for 24 hours prior to fitment. Many newer replacement bearings can be fitted immediately.

Pre-engaged unit in situ; this is a classic Ford tractor, most starters are not so accessible.

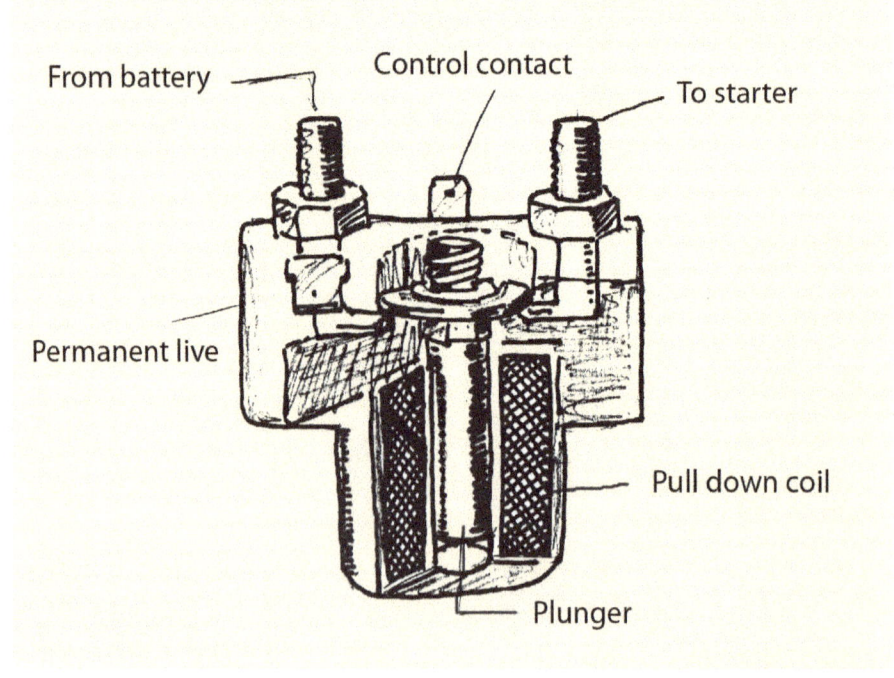

Inside the solenoid.

Remove pinion
The pinion set is usually held together with heavy circlips and a roll-pin. To remove the retainers, which secure the pinion set, you will need to compress the springs, which may require the use of a press. Take care to note the position of the various springs and spacers of your particular device – I would suggest photographing it first.

The simplest option is to acquire an exchange or new unit.

The tests used to check the Starter motor are detailed below, as they are common to both types of unit.

THE STARTER MOTOR

The starter solenoid
The solenoid is the heavy-duty switch which is used to control the current to the starter motor. It is controlled by the ignition switch and is deployed only for the time that the starter is actually running. In practice, the solenoid is pretty reliable and long lived, it is pretty simple to test but a fault usually means replacement.

Earlier starter solenoids and those used with automatic vehicles are closed, while those found on most '60s and '70s cars can usually be used as remote starters as they feature a button on top which manually closes the main contacts. See tests below.

The pre-engaged starter motor
The pre-engaged starter is now the norm and can commonly be found on vehicles from the mid-seventies onward. The obvious difference is that the solenoid is mounted piggyback on the motor and doubles as current switch and pinion launcher.

Unlike the earlier type solenoid, the later units will tend to have two coils one to 'pull-down' and one to 'hold-down'.

The mechanism used to deploy the pinion is basically a lever, which is pulled by the solenoid plunger. The pinion itself has a one-way clutch, which prevents damage to the motor as the engine spins-up.

The pre-engaged unit is less likely to stick than its earlier cousin, and as the pinion is positively engaged before the motor spins, up it is less likely to have worn teeth. On the occasions when the thing does stick, the procedure is the same as for the earlier device (see above).

In essence the motor section is much the same as for the earlier machine, though very modern units are more likely to have brushes set at the rear of the commutator, as opposed to being mounted on the sides. You can expect to find four brushes, of which two will normally be linked together and the other pair attached to the field contacts.

Removal from car
Removing the starter from the car is fairly straightforward, and well within the scope of the average home mechanic. The car must be made secure and the battery earth disconnected to prevent shorting.

Typically the motor body will be fixed to the bell-housing by two or three bolts, one of which may enter from the rear. You may also find a locating peg, this will demand that the unit is withdrawn away from its place as opposed to dropped. If the motor is reluctant to come away then a sharp tap from a copper mallet should

The ford RS 2000 starter is bolted to a bellhousing, and is accessed from under the vehicle.

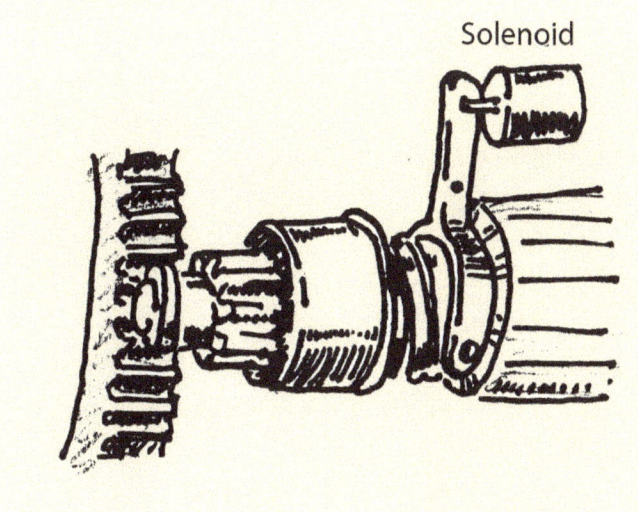
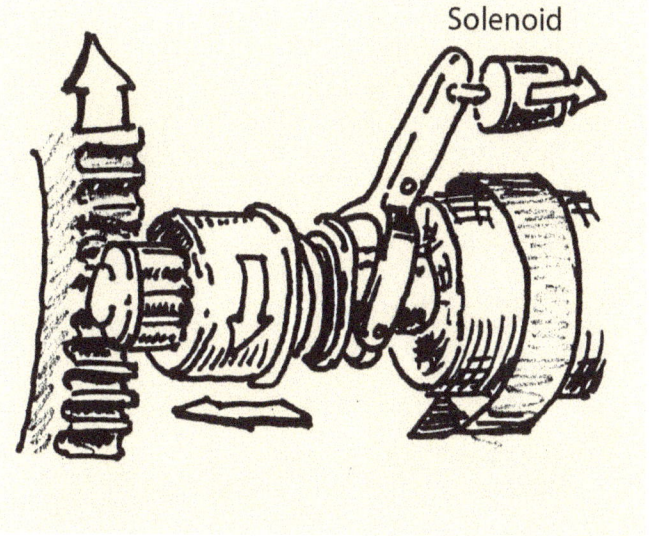

Pre-engaged starter and solenoid operation.

ENTHUSIAST'S RESTORATION MANUAL SERIES

help; be careful though, as, like the inertia starter, it is rather heavy!

Some vehicles, notably the VW Golf range, will feature a bush bearing at the end of the starter motor shaft. This will be left in the bell housing after the motor is extracted. Remove it using a treading tap. A new bush will be supplied with the overhaul kit or exchange motor. Although it is very tempting not to bother with it, don't skimp here.

Cleaning the pinion set

Any dust or oil can be cleaned off with petrol applied on a paintbrush, but be careful not to let this enter the motor body. Thoroughly dry before refitting. Never oil or grease the pinion as this will encourage sticking. At most, a little pencil-lead can be used as a lubricant.

Dismantling

Every unit will be different and I cannot stress the usefulness of owners clubs and the like at this point in time.

Basically the procedure for dismantling the pre-engaged starter is to undo the electrical connection between the solenoid and the motor, before removing the solenoid itself – which is usually attached to the common fixing bracket by two bolts. The solenoid should then be free to be extracted with a wiggle from the lever.

Dismantling the lever and pinion set

It seems to me that the real problem with this sort of device is that without great care it will all go 'ping', and you will have bits all over the place! Again, I cannot stress enough that the exact procedure will vary from unit to unit, but if you are the sort of person who is comfortable with dismantling this sort of thing then, be it on your head. It ain't rocket science, but getting it wrong can be a headache – and may cost a tad more!

THE STARTER MOTOR TESTS
In car tests
1. Battery

The simplest test for a faulty starter is to turn off the engine and switch on your headlights, if the lights come on bright, but quickly dim, then the battery is suspect.

If, on the other hand, the lights stay bright, then the battery is good and the cause of your problem lies elsewhere.

2. Cables and connections

The first check for the starter system itself should always be a good visual and hands-on inspection of all the connections. A rusty earth-lead or mounting point can easily spoil the car's ability to start. Stress fracturing or overheating of cable near to a connection is common but not always easy to spot. If in doubt, remove any cable from the car and clean it up; stress fractures or brittleness caused by heat might be felt as either a loose or crumbly section of cable.

Peace of mind and better starting for the price of a new cable? What a bargain!

Now disable your ignition! The next group of tests are best performed if the car cannot fire-up accidentally. Remove the feed to the ignition coil. Don't forget to put it back later.

Listen and feel. Turn to key, does the solenoid kick-in with a healthy 'crack'? Does the starter sound anaemic? Does it spin-up every time, or does is it a bit unpredictable?

If the battery is healthy and the

Disconnect the coil feed wire to disable the ignition when testing the starter motor.

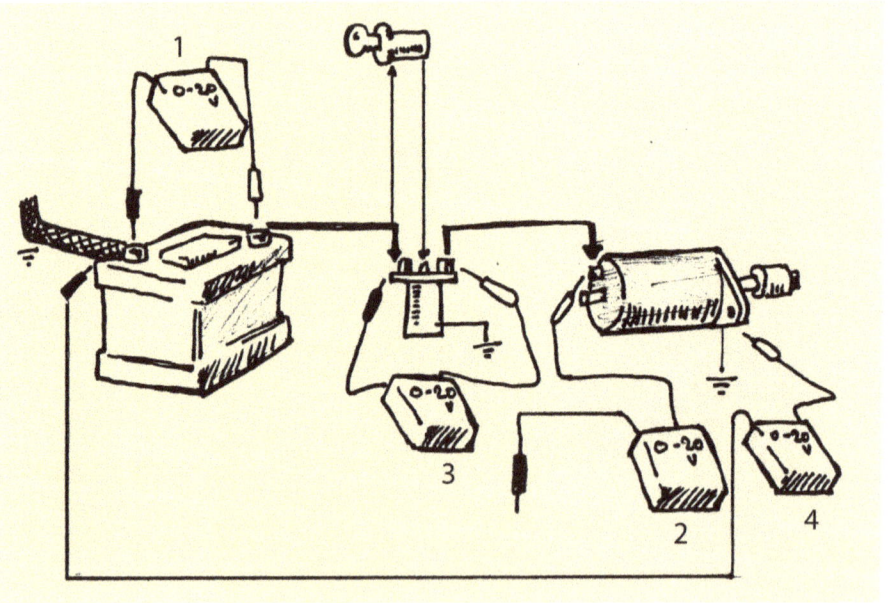

Starter motor tests using voltage meter.

THE STARTER MOTOR

connections appear good, then it is time to get the test-gear out.

If the starter is not turning, then either the unit is completely knackered or the voltage is blocked somewhere down the line. A simple live-tester or test lamp connected between various points along the system and a good earth will show you where the power is. From this you will see where the power isn't.

A bridge of wire can be used to temporarily connect across the contacts of the solenoid, this would feed the motor and show up problems in the solenoid or its control.

You might also use a heavy cable to provide a makeshift earth return from the motor to the battery.

3. Volt-meter tests
Use a meter set to 0-20V with clips on the cables, and it might help to have another person turn the key.

1. Battery voltage. Place the volt-meter across the battery terminals and turn the starter over. Under starting load you would expect to see a reading of about 10V – we will call it 10.5V for now as it makes the explanation of the next bit easier.

2. Motor terminal voltage. Connect the volt-meter between the input terminal of the starter motor and a good earth – such as the motor body. When the motor is run you should get a reading within 0.5V of the previous value. Thus if you had 10.5V across the battery then you need to see not less than 10V now. Any less and there is some extra resistance in the system. This may be the solenoid contacts or possibly the actual motor current circuit.

3. The solenoid can be checked by placing the volt-meter between its contacts. With the system at rest, the reading should show battery voltage. With the motor running, you should have a meter reading of zero, if not then clean or replace the solenoid.

4. Earth test. Set the volt-meter between the motor body and the battery negative terminal (positive if the system is positive earth). Under starting load you should get a reading of zero. This test can also be used across the earth lead.

Voltage test across battery terminals.

4. Starter motor out tests
Before any dismantling, it is worth hooking the motor up to a 12V supply and seeing how it spins. Be certain to hold the motor securely and connect it to the battery by heavy cables. The motor should spin into life with a kick, rather than just rotate gently. Repeat this test a few times, as a single faulty segment on the commutator might not show up immediately.

If you do dismantle the motor, check for signs of burning on the rotor windings, this would suggest a faulty coil. And the need to replace the unit.

The field windings can be checked for continuity with either a meter or with a battery and test lamp. Connect the meter or lamp/battery to either end of the section to be checked – if the current passes from one end to the other that is good, but it does not rule out shorting to the case.

Repeat the test with the feed as before but take the return off the casing. If the lamp lights or the meter shows a current then the winding is shorted and the unit needs replacing. You can find specialists, who can replace windings, but for most cars this is not an economical approach.

Even the most exotic of machines tend to have starters and the like supplied by big companies, names like Lucas, FoMoco, and Delco, Paris-Rhone, etc will pop up repeatedly. Contact them directly or through your owners club.

Chapter 12
The ignition system

The key to running a classic car is correct and regular maintenance of its ignition system. Failure or negligence in this department will only reward you with unreliability.

Even in their day, the cars we now treasure did not perform nearly as consistently as the modern counterparts which we often think of as characterless.

My wife's Toyota may be dull, but it has never let her down, and that is more than I can say for my Imp, Anglia, Herald, Mini, or any of the other 'interesting' cars that I have ever owned. It behoves us, then, to become familiar with the workings of the ignition system and its component parts. It will also pay dividends to read up on your own vehicle's peculiarities.

Every one of the system's components play their part in generating and delivering the spark, so any minor deficiency can result in major problems.

THE COIL

The ignition coil is actually two coils sited one inside the other. In this respect it might be considered as a 'transformer'.

The outer LT or low tension (low-voltage or primary) coil is fed from the battery and is connected to the contact-breaker. The HT or high tension (high-voltage or secondary) coil is situated inside the LT coil and is made-up of many thousands of turns of wire. The ratio of turns between the LT and HT coils will govern the voltage produced on the HT side.

The complete ignition system.

This old Riley twin cam has modern electrics and an un-ballasted coil fixed to the bulkhead.

THE IGNITION SYSTEM

The LT side is connected to the distributor via the king-lead which supplies the sparking current. The HT side will produce about 30,000 volts – dependent on the age of the vehicle – which is high enough to jump the plug-gap, and so ignite the fuel/air mixture.

Later and larger classics are often fitted with a 6V coil. On such systems a ballast resistor is used to reduce the voltage during normal running. The resistor is bypassed at start-up to increase the power.

Long-lived vehicles such as the MGB started life with a 12V coil, but received a 6V unit in later years. The two coils are not interchangeable, at least not without fitment of the rest of the appropriate wiring.

How it works

The windings of the ignition coil surround a soft iron core, this has the effect of concentrating the magnetic field, which is produced when current flows through the LT side and on to the closed contact-breaker, from where it runs to earth.

When the contact-breaker is opened, the magnetic field in the LT coil collapses and, in so doing, induces a high-voltage current in the secondary side. This then is the HT used in ignition.

It is very rare for a coil to be supplied from a fused source, if the coil is not being fed, then the problem will lie with the key switch.

THE DISTRIBUTOR

The job of the distributor is to time and distribute the spark. The distributor body is a mechanical device which houses a shaft that is turned by the engine at half of crank speed; this is to account for the fact that the cylinders need to fire only on each second revolution.

A worn distributor gear or shaft will require replacement and is primarily a mechanical job, however, anyone undertaking such work needs to consider the implications to the electrical system. Make certain that the distributor is replaced correctly with relation to timing.

The distributor cap is generally thought of as a consumable. It protects the internals of the distributor from the elements and holds the contact points for the individual sparkplug leads. It also holds the leads themselves. In the centre of the cap is the king-lead contact, which is commonly made of sprung carbon. As the contacts are prone to wear and spark-erosion, as well as 'tracking*', a spare cap in the tool-box is a good idea.

*Tracking is the name given to tiny cracks, which will short the HT to earth, these often only show up as tracks when they are blackened with carbon dust.

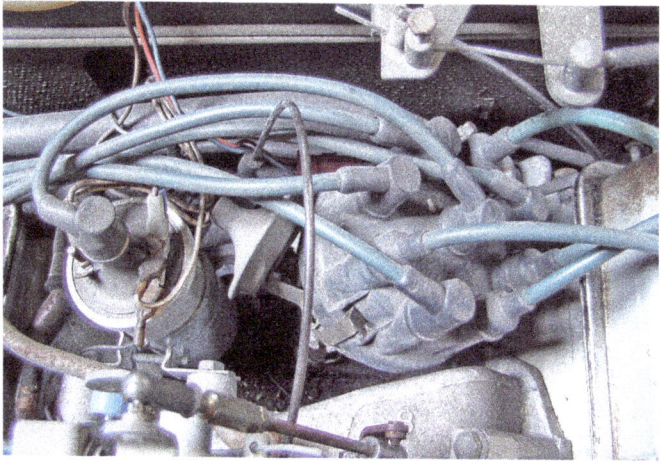

V8 distributor as fitted to Triumph Stag. Sport models of this car featured twin contact breakers.

Ballast resistor means that this system runs at 6V. The resistor is by-passed at start-up.

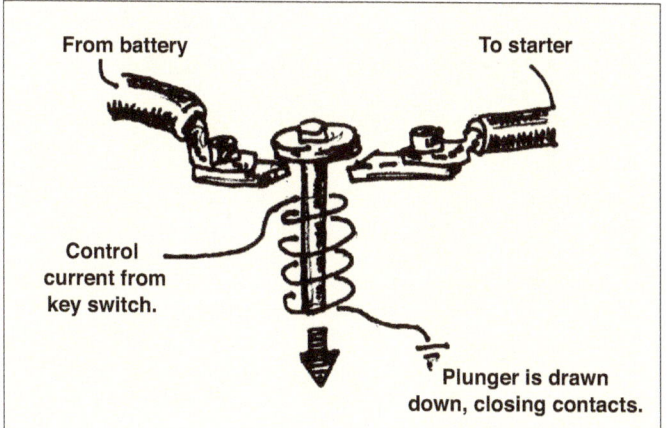

Principles of the starter solenoid.

The rotor arm is easily cleaned or replaced.

55

ENTHUSIAST'S RESTORATION MANUAL SERIES

THE ROTOR-ARM
The rotor-arm is another consumable, it is the moving contact which bridges between the central king-lead and the individual plug-leads.

THE CONTACT-BREAKER
The contact-breaker, or 'points' as they are often referred to, is sited within the distributor. Essentially the contact-breaker is a switch that is operated by a lobed cam on the shaft. While the switch is closed, current runs through the coils LT side. When the cam opens the contacts, the magnetic-field in the coil collapses inducing a current in the HT side. To prevent sparking across the points a condenser is fitted, this can be thought of as a rather short-lived battery – it soaks up any stray current and spits it out again later. This is why condensers or capacitors are used to reduce radio interference.

The degree to which the contact-breaker points open is critical and is set with a feeler gauge. The exact time that the points open is also of vital importance and is set by moving the rotor body relative to the shaft. This can be performed whilst the engine is running EI dynamically or with the engine still EI static (see below).

The period during which the contact points are closed is when the charge is created and is called the dwell . And as it can be regarded as fraction of the rotors turn, it is Often referred to as the Dwell-angle. Too short, or too long a dwell will result in a poor spark.

Dedicated automotive multi-meter scan measure the dwell angel accurately.

As a matter course you should try to keep everything in the distributor clean and dry. Regular cleaning of the electrical contacts is essential as they are prone to furring up. Any dirt interfering with the contact-breaker will reduce performance. –'A goodly squirt of WD40 followed by a wipe around,- can cure all known ills!'

THE HT LEADS
The HT leads are the high voltage cables that feed the distributor and sparkplugs.

The condition of the HT leads is critical, any break in the insulation will quickly lead to a misfire as the charge is run prematurely to earth. Likewise any break in the conductor would produce unsatisfactory performance.

'Earthing' from the leads is normally heard as a rhythmic 'crack'crack'crack', and is easily seen in darkness -as the power jumps in the form of a spark to any handy metalwork.

Keep the leads clean and dry, the rubber end caps should seal out the elements. Many people shy away from replacing the leads when carrying out a service, simply because; "They're, just wires, they look all right!" A new set of leads can make all the difference, don't skimp here.

THE SPARKPLUGS
The sparkplugs have the job of producing a spark from the pulses of high voltage produced by the coil. The most obvious feature of the plugs is that they are made largely from porcelain, which is a very good insulator. This, of course, is to keep the current from running or jumping to earth prematurely.

New plug and correct gapping tool.

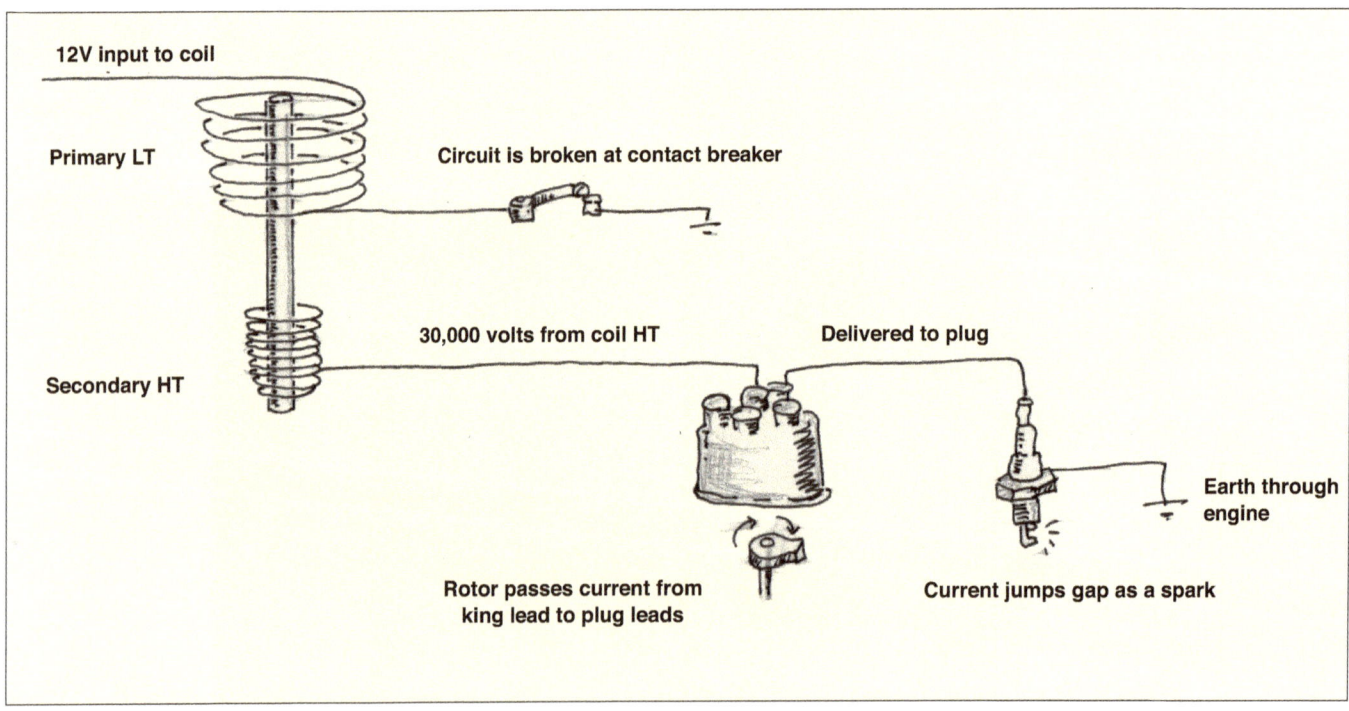

THE IGNITION SYSTEM

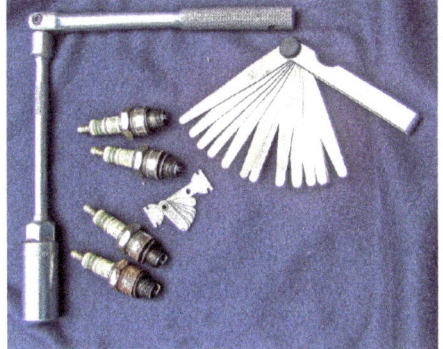

Plugs and the proper tools for the job.

The size of the plug gap is critical to good running and must be correctly set and maintained.

In normal use it is in the nature of the sparkplug to become furred, fouled and eroded. A tired, oily or poorly tuned, engine will only exacerbate this situation.

Back in the sixties and seventies a set of plugs was reckoned to last a year, it was recommended then that sparkplugs be cleaned every three thousand miles, on a well maintained engine. I cannot speak for the state of your motor, but I think a new set of plugs is a good idea when giving a car its annual service. That said, many of

The multi-electrode plug is an attempt to improve combustion.

our classics will not do many miles. If the plugs look good, then they probably are.

Any fouling or deposit on the plugs will tell its own story – oil and soot are self-

Awkward and deep-set plugs are easily broken. Only ever use the correct tools.

explanatory, while erosion or breakage will mean replacement. Glazing is a sign of too much heat. A healthy plug should show a fine white/grey powdery coating.

Proprietary tools are available for adjusting the electrode gap and are always preferable to bouncing the things off the floor (a technique I have seen employed many many times).

Always clean around the plugs with a paintbrush or air line before removal, and use a correctly fitting plug-spanner or socket. Be careful not to over-tighten;

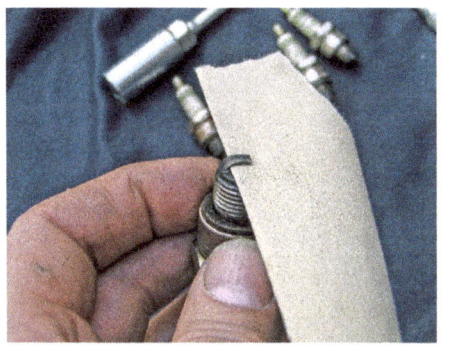

Cleaning plug electrode with abrasive paper.

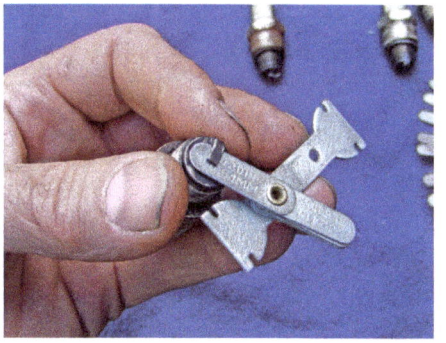

Measuring and adjusting the plug gap with the correct tool – don't tap them on the floor to gap them!

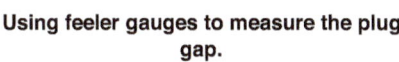

Using feeler gauges to measure the plug gap.

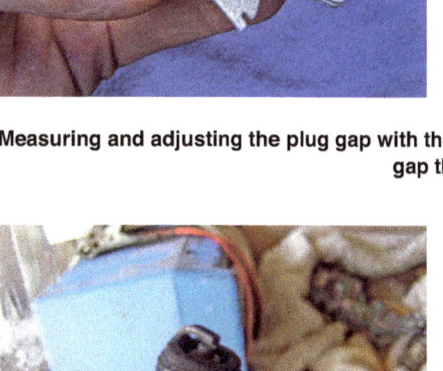

A sooty plug suggests poor burning – is it the mixture? Choke? Timing? Or burnt oil?

An oily plug from the same car caused rough running.

57

ENTHUSIAST'S RESTORATION MANUAL SERIES

most plugs now come with a compression washer to create the seal.

Loose plugs are a liability and may strip themselves out – a fine smear of oil or copper ease on the plug threads will make fitment easier.

To facilitate fitting really awkward or deep set plugs, you can try slipping the end into a length of 3/8in rubber hose. Use the hose as a universal joint, if you foul-thread the thing, the hose will tend to slip before any damage occurs.

In the event of a stripped thread you will need to fit a thread insert; these are widely available and not too tricky – but remember to remove every little bit of swarf and grit from inside the cylinder.

A typical plug gap measures 0.64mm (0.025in).

THE IGNITION TESTS
There are many simple tests for the ignition system. Most do not require any specialist equipment, but they all demand common sense, and a healthy respect for the 30,000V which feeds the spark.

If you are working with the ignition live, then use insulated pliers and screwdrivers.

It is not always possible to see tracking, and a component such as a distributor cap, which in theory will not give you a shock, just might.

Caution! – Working near the fan and pulleys is another specific hazard, while using the strobe will make the fast-moving parts appear stationary or, worse, invisible. Be warned.

It is normal to start at the plugs and work backward toward the switch. Unless you have a suspicion as to where your problem lies, stick with this strategy. Before you get into any detective work you must eliminate the possibility of dirt, water, or loose connections, as the cause of your trouble. A simple hands-on once-over of all the leads may improve things, as might a quick clean-up of the distributor contacts. Only having ruled out the simple should you now proceed with the diagnostic tests below.

When carrying out any checks which involve the ignition, you should try to avoid leaving the coil energised unnecessarily as it may tend to get hot and damaged.

THE HT LEADS AND PLUGS
If you suspect that one of the cylinders is not firing, the easiest way to determine which one is at fault is to remove one HT lead at a time and then run the engine. Removal of the lead which feeds the plug which is not firing will make no difference to the misfire. Removal of a good lead will make things run worse.

To test the individual lead you can disconnect it from its plug and set it in a position where the end is close to good earth (ideally about 3mm/1/8in). If you now turn over the engine, a healthy spark should jump from the end of the lead to earth.

I would not advise anyone to hold the lead while carrying out this test; special pliers are available for this sort of thing, as are light-up gadgets which interpose between lead and sparkplug. If the lead appears to be working then the individual plugs can be removed and tested in much the same way.

Set the plug into the lead and place it in close proximity to a good earth and then turn the engine as before: a spark should be seen to jump the gap between the electrodes or the earth.

If no spark is found at any of the HT leads, then it is worth performing the same test on the king-lead. Remove the lead from the centre of the distributor and place the end close to a good earth, turn over the engine and look for a spark.

If no spark is present then the problem may lie in the contact-breaker or the coil itself.

If the king-lead does spark then you must suspect the distributor cap or rotor-arm.

To test the central contact king-post of the cap, you can place a heavy screwdriver to short between the contact and a good earth on the engine, leaving a gap near the contact for the spark to jump. As you might guess, getting this one wrong can give you a shock from the ignition, and I would think twice before performing it.

The easiest way to test the coil is to replace it with a good one and see what happens. A faulty coil may only present itself when warmed up, which can make diagnosis tricky.

Continuity across the coil's primary LT can be tested with an ohmmeter or a test lamp.

CONTACT-BREAKER
Using a 12V test lamp or live-tester, you can check if the contact-breaker is being supplied with current.

With the distributor cap off, look to see if the contact-breaker is actually opening by turning over the engine. If a spark can be seen across the contact-breaker points, then the condenser is in need of replacement or your contacts are dirty. Pitting or burning of the contacts is a sign of excessive sparking and suggests a faulty condenser. Clean the points with a bit of fine abrasive paper or a disposable nail file – I nick them from the wife.

If the feed to the contact-breaker is good, but no spark is present, then touch the positive of the live-tester to the earth side of the contact-breaker and turn the engine over. It will not fire as the cap is off.

As the contacts open, the tester should flash off. If the lamp stays on then the contacts are not breaking the circuit.

If the points do not open then adjust them to the correct gap (see below).

V12 supercar has twin ignition systems.

THE IGNITION SYSTEM

The cam is at the apex but the gap is closed, so no spark will be generated.

Slacken the base plate screw.

Pry open the gap – you will often find lugs to help with this.

Replacing the contact-breaker

The contact-breaker consists of a fixed contact, a spring-loaded moving contact and a condenser. I would suggest that all three be replaced as one job. The fixed contact or point is actually the one we adjust during servicing.

Remove the cap and carefully remove the condenser followed by the points. The condenser is often fixed by a nut to the distributor body, while the points are usually screwed to a base plate which sits above the advance mechanism. On some models the base plate will require removal, which will demand disconnection from the vacuum body. This is normally just a hook or simple link.

Be certain to clean any washers etc and replace all parts in the correct order. This is one of those jobs which is easier to do, than to describe.

Later models will have a 'one piece' contact-breaker set which, as the name suggests, is fitted as one unit.

CONTACT-BREAKER POINTS GAP

To set the gap requires a set of feeler-gauges and a flat-bladed screwdriver. You will also need to know the correct gap setting. Typically 0.35-0.4mm/0.014-0.016in. If you can't find your own spec, try this in an emergency ...

Remove the distributor cap and turn the engine so that the contacts open fully. This can be done by putting the car in gear and then rolling it while watching the shaft turn. This method is only suitable for manual cars and those of you with a safe flat area to work on.

The alternative is to use an appropriate sized socket on the crank pulley to turn the engine – do this with the car in neutral and the ignition disabled. Removing the plugs makes it easier. Yet another method is to 'blip' the key switch until the shaft stops at the correct place – this is the lazy way, and a bit hit and miss.

When the cam is at its apex, simple place the feeler gauge in place and slacken the base plate screw until the fixed contact

A feeler gauge used to determine the gap.

can be 'tweaked' to the correct place, relative to the (now open) moving contact.

A pair of lugs is often provide, and these allow for ease of adjustment by means of a screwdriver which is twisted between them. When the appropriate size of feeler can be slid 'snuggly' between the contacts, the base plate is tightened and the job is done. But don't forget to remove that socket on the crank pulley.

TIMING THE IGNITION

There are basically two methods of timing the ignition: one – the static method – is fairly simple and is 'good enough'; the other – the dynamic method – is more complicated but more precise. If the drive to the distributor is worn, then static timing may prove unreliable.

Timing marks

Both methods require specific knowledge of the engines timing and timing marks.

As you know it is essential for the

The cam at the apex and gap is correct.

detonation to occur at the correct point in the piston's cycle. This point is given relative to the number 1 cylinder at 'top dead centre' or TDC. This is to say, when the piston is at the highest point immediately prior to the power stroke. To aid timing, the manufacturer will give

Ignition timing marks on a VW crank pulley.

59

ENTHUSIAST'S RESTORATION MANUAL SERIES

Timing marks may be found on the flywheel.

a mark or set of marks on either the crank pulley or flywheel. Commonly you will find a mark for TDC and scale calibrated in degrees, shown as BTDC or 'before top dead centre', this may continue to ATDC in some cases. It will be helpful to clean the marks and maybe even highlight them with a little white paint or typist correction fluid.

For the static method you will require a test lamp and a few simple hand tools. The dynamic method also calls for a stroboscopic timing lamp. This need not be expensive – but I would avoid the very cheapest. The better ones use power from the battery to amplify the light, making the job so much easier.

Static timing

In a four-stroke engine, the pulley will align with its mark twice in the cycle – so it is necessary for us to determine when number 1 cylinder is ready to fire. To do this you can either remove the valve-cover and watch for both valves to be shut, or you can faff about with a finger in the sparkplug hole, feeling for the compression.

With the cap off, set the engine so that number 1 is at, or very near, TDC using the mark and the position of the rotor. Place your test lamp or live-tester across the two LT terminals of the coil. Slacken off the clamp bolt that secures the distributor body enough so that it may be turned.

The very point at which the lamp goes out corresponds to the opening of the contact-breaker points, and we need this to occur at the exact same time as the pulley aligns to the fixed timing mark.

When the lamp and the mark coincide, you should tighten the clamp bolt.

Unfortunately there is not really such a thing as a typical static timing value, and most cars will be timed to between 2 and 10 degrees BTDC, which is quite a margin.

Having used this method, you may find it helpful to now run the car at idle and 'tweak' the position of the distributor. Generally, the nearer it is to correct, the faster and smoother the car will run. This isn't very scientific but it does work – usually!

If your particular model is fitted with a vernier or fine adjuster, then the final 'tweak' is made using this.

Dynamic timing with a stroboscope

The dynamic method of timing is more precise and better suited to engines that are a bit tired.

The strobe light is triggered by number 1 sparkplug and is, therefore, synchronised to it. By shining the lamp onto the timing marks we can make them appear still, and if the marks align correctly then the timing is spot-on. Any mis-register is corrected by adjusting the distributor in much the same way as above.

Set the car in neutral and make certain that the brake is applied. Set the timing light in circuit with number 1 plug and connect the power leads to the battery (as per manufacturers instructions). Be careful to place all leads in a safe position away from any parts which will shortly be moving.

Highlight the timing marks and consider how best to see the marks and adjust the distributor when the engine is in motion without danger. Slacken off the distributor clamp, and disconnect the vacuum advance pipe and plug it.

Run the engine at about 700rpm and check the timing against its marks – this may be easier if the engine is allowed to warm up as uneven running may result in the timing drifting a small amount.

Make large adjustments by rotating the distributor. Any fine tweaking is best done utilising the vernier (if fitted).

Remember to re-tighten the clamp.

If you are not happy to fiddle with a engine while it is running, then you can always turn it off, make the adjustment and try again. Better safe than sorry.

A live-tester shows exactly when the contact breaker opens.

Stroboscope. This is synchronised with number 1 sparkplug.

THE IGNITION SYSTEM

Timing marks lit up under strobe lighting.

The ignition advance mechanisms should be cleaned using a light oil such as WD40, any grit or rust must be removed from the area or it will foul up the works.

You will often find a felt pad under the rotor-arm, this needs to be oiled regularly, and a fine spread of light grease on the lobes of the cam will reduce wear.

UPGRADING THE IGNITION SYSTEM

Back in the seventies and eighties it was fairly common for the more go-ahead of motorists to improve the ignition system. As such, many of the improvements might be considered as 'period' and you may wish to try them.

Modern plugs and leads are superior to the original and many of us will use them as a matter of course.

Transistor assisted contact or TAC ignition systems – which are effectively add-ons – have the advantage of prolonging the life of the contact-breaker by reducing the voltage load across it. This particular type of device also allows for an uprated coil giving you better starting and a more efficient burn – can't be bad.

Sadly as the electronic ignition has become standard on new cars, so the market for TAC systems has gone and they are now difficult to find.

CONTACT-BREAKERLESS IGNITIONS

Another option, which is fairly discrete, is the optical chopper type of rotor. Popularly known as the 'Lumenition' system, this device, which links neatly with a transistor package, is hidden inside the distributor. The system works by replacing the contact-breaker points with an LED and a photo-diode, the beam of which

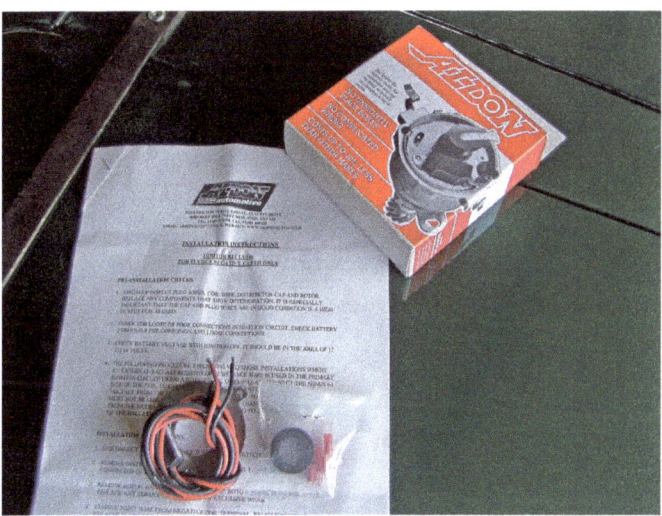

The 'Aldon Ignitor' as it arrived.

The new unit is easily swapped for the original as it uses the same base mounting.

21st century reliability from a car which is half a century old.

is interrupted by a set of rotating vanes. The individual vanes correspond exactly to the timing of the contacts opening and closing. Because they are pre-set, they will always be correct, so, in theory, once installed the device never needs adjusting, and benefits from the the fact that dwell will remain constant at all speeds, and the thing is immune to damp. And as these improvements have been around for many years, many of us can fit them without giving up on originality ... which is nice.

More recently, specialist oufits such as Aldon, have produced a discreet electronic system for a wide range of older cars. The 'Ignitor' is easily fitted in place of the contact-breaker and consists of a new base plate onto which is mounted a sensor module, and a ring which slips over the distributor shaft. Within the ring are four magnets which trigger the ignition. The net result is modern reliability from your old motor, and the capacity to run a hotter coil. The system costs about £100 all up.

Note – transistorised systems do not like being jump-started, as a completely flat battery cannot act as a damper for the output of the slave car. Invest in a surge protector.

The exact specification for your model will be of enormous help.

Chapter 13
Lighting

Since the early days of motoring, it has been common practice for car manufacturers to buy-in lighting components from specialist suppliers. Throughout the sixties and seventies the type of round lamps shown here were all but ubiquitous. Design trends in the eighties and advances in production led to bespoke lamps being fitted to different cars. Today it is rare to see the same lamp on two different models, even within the same stable.

Your headlamps will be fed through a fuse, either as a pair or individually. Here, then (apart from the bulbs themselves), is the first place to look should your lights fail. The switch gear is unlikely to give trouble, but when dealing with an aged car we can rule out nothing.

The most common problems we will encounter with our lighting are earthing faults and poor connections, which are usually caused by water ingress. The actual connectors are generally of the self-cleaning variety, so simply removing and re-fitting the spade or plug may well improve things.

Where the earth lead runs to the bodywork, you will often find corrosion which will impede the electrical flow. Five minutes spent cleaning up the rust may be more profitable than an hour's investigation with a probe. Remember that just because the live-tester shows a voltage, it does not necessarily mean that there is enough power to light up the lamp.

The other problem you will encounter

The humble Escort and ...

... the iconic E-type ...

... share the same headlamps as the mighty DB5.

is 'history' or, more specifically, all the previous owners and people who have tinkered with your car. Don't be too surprised to find wires which have been chopped and taped or stuck together with chewing-gum.

Be prepared to sort out any and all bodges, as they do not improve with time!

THE HEADLAMPS

The vast majority of domestic classics from the period that concerns us will be fitted with standard headlamp units. These will usually be of the sealed-beam or semi-sealed (ordinary) type, which I am sure are fairly familiar to all of us. Both of these will include one filament for dipped, and another for high beam. Non standard headlamps will not be too dissimilar in make up and the following will apply to them also.

ENTHUSIAST'S RESTORATION MANUAL SERIES

The sealed beam unit is essentially a large bulb.

The rear of the sealed beam unit shows contacts.

A semi-sealed unit looks similar ...

... but reveals a hole for a separate bulb.

The sealed-beam unit is effectively a very large pre-focused bulb, with its own reflector.

The semi-sealed unit looks much the same, but has a large hole in the back into which a separate pre-focused bulb is set.

This type of lamp would originally have been suspended in an adjustable frame and mounted into a steel backing-bowl, sited in an aperture in the wing or front panel. Later models use a plastic bowl

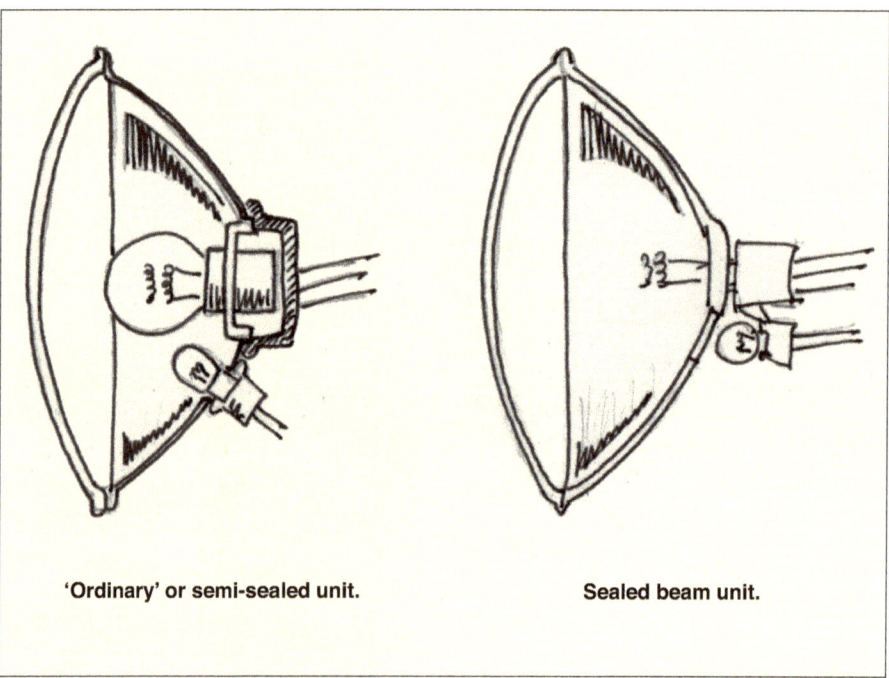

'Ordinary' or semi-sealed unit.

Sealed beam unit.

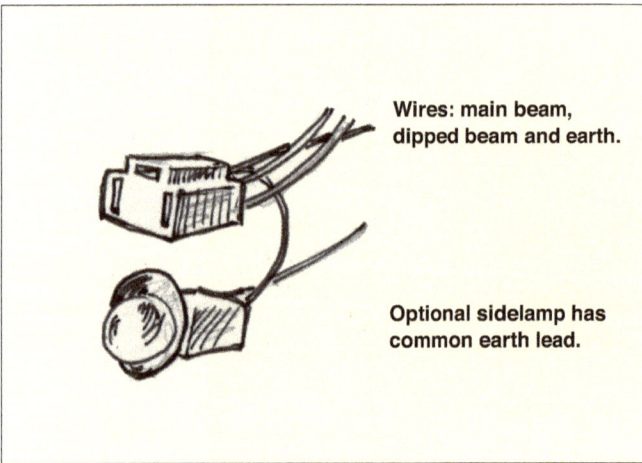

Wires: main beam, dipped beam and earth.

Optional sidelamp has common earth lead.

Headlamp plug connector.

Mk3 Cortina double lamps – the inner units are high beam.

LIGHTING

Headlamp and bezel – this one comes from a Triumph Herald.

The bezel removed, revealing retaining ring and lamp adjusting screws.

The ring is removed by undoing three very rusty screws which often break.

The lamp is lifted out ...

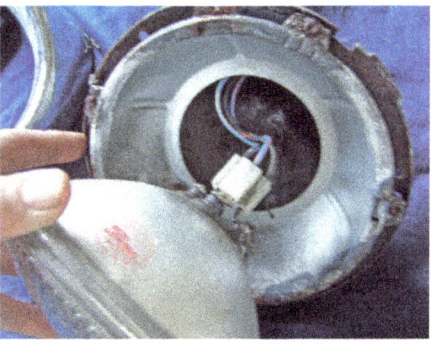

... to reveal a push fit connector.

This particular lamp has a clear section to allow for separate side light bulb.

which, of course, doesn't rust. The plastic type bowl has long been used to replace most rotten originals. So much so that even the purist will not frown on this upgrade.

The chrome ring or bezel appears on vast numbers of automobiles, though as time went on, the headlamp moved from the wing to the front panel. As such, later cars will often lose the bezel in favour of the front grille

Four headlamps?
On many models which feature a four-headlamp design, you will find that the inner pair act as high beam only. In such cases, be certain to fit lamps and bulbs correctly.

Replacement of a sealed-beam unit
To replace a sealed-beam unit we must first remove the chrome bezel or trim. The bezel is usually held in place by a set of tabs and a single screw located centrally under the ring. On some models you will find wire springs which are used to hold the bezel in tension, while others will rely on a rubber gasket to do this job. Removal of the bezel will usually reveal three clamping screws and three adjusting screws. Before attempting to turn any of them, a quick

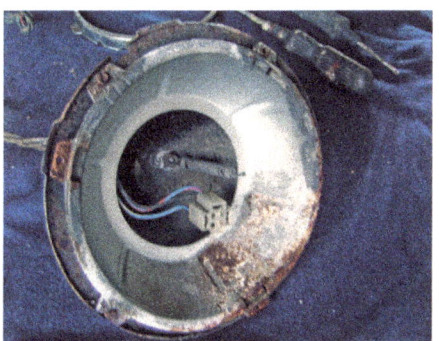

Lamp holder and adjusting mechanism.

squirt of WD40 is a good idea as they are rather prone to snapping off.

The headless adjusters articulate in swivel mountings which on earlier lamps would have been metal, these are more usually now plastic. Again, the metal type tend to rust away, and fitment of the later type is seen as acceptable.

Removal of the clamp screws will allow removal of the glass which is heavy and, if not supported, may drop and smash. The electrical plug on the rear of the unit can now be disconnected. Fitting a new unit is simply the process in reverse.

The original metal bowl – these rust terribly.

Semi-sealed units
The semi-sealed unit looks pretty much the same as the sealed-beam, but has a hole at the back to allow bulbs to be replaced. Because the lamp is accessed from behind, many headlights of this type are mounted in such a way as to make removal of the unit itself unnecessary or downright difficult. The manufacturer should have allowed for bulb replacement, though don't be surprised if you need to remove a battery or something to gain access.

Because this type of lamp is not enclosed, it is normal to find a rubber cover

65

ENTHUSIAST'S RESTORATION MANUAL SERIES

Rusty lamp holders benefit from a coat of red oxide primer.

The bulb holder and cover are clearly seen.

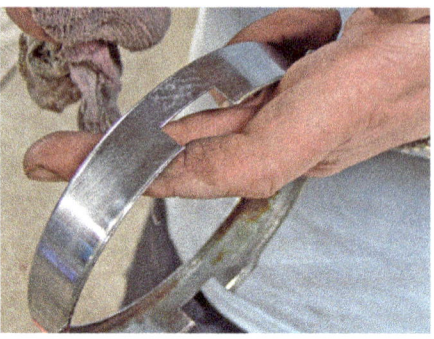
The retaining ring is cleaned with a little WD40 on a cloth.

The lamp holder is given a coat of Hammerite ...

... before mounting it on the car and refitting the grille.

This MG T is original in every detail.

or seal around the contacts and aperture. Various spring-clip and bayonet type fixtures, are used to hold the bulb in place.

Avoid handling the glass 'envelope' of the bulb and be sure to fit it the correct way up! Most fittings will have a notch to help correct location.

Due to their location, the headlamps and their mountings are under constant attack from the elements. It pays to keep the contacts and adjusters clean and lubricated. A little petorleum jelly can be used to keep water off the contacts, but must not be allowed to interfere with the electrical joint. Ensure that the spades are tight.

This cheekily chopped 1957 Riley sports huge Lancia lamps which have been adapted to use standard units.

A cute Morgan 3 wheeler.

LIGHTING

Earlier headlamps
Earlier vehicles may feature headlamps which are dipped by means of a solenoid. The same mechanism will often extinguish the main fillament.

Shown here is a lovely old Morgan with original headlamps, and a cheekily chopped '57 Riley, which has been fitted with huge lamps (originally from a Lancia). These have been adapted to take sealed-beam units. The owner tells me that "being able to see, is quite important!"

STOP, TAIL, AND SIDELIGHTS

Brake lights and side markers tend to suffer from the effects of water ingress even more than the headlamps, and vehicles from the fifties and early sixties commonly feature standard bullet shaped lamps. These units are still available off-the-shelf today, though will now come with plastic lenses as opposed to the heavy glass originals.

Numberplate lamps are required at the rear of the vehicle, and these should light up with the side markers.

More specialised lamps will also be found, and will generally be made up of:

Lens – this may be of glass or plastic, and might be fabricated in sections of various colours.

Reflector – this will be metal on earlier models, but in chromed-plastic on later designs, and may or may not be part of the ...

Backing plate – this is used to close the lamp, hold the bulbs, and to attach the unit to the body.

DeLorean – a real classic?

The E-type shares lamps with the Daimler limo.

This humble MGB has bespoke lamps ...

... unlike the 250 GTO which has 'off the shelf' units.

67

ENTHUSIAST'S RESTORATION MANUAL SERIES

Seal or gasket – sealing the lamp from the elements is crucial to the good working of the lamp. Tired of perished seals will need renewing.

Maintenance of brake and sidelamps

Many designs will allow access to the bulbs by simple removal of the lens. Lamps which show screws are usually mounted from the outside of the bodywork.

Models which do not give a clue to their attachment will need to be unbolted from somewhere behind the panel. A generous squirt of WD40 or similar the day before attempting to undo aged fixings would be wise, as they are prone to breaking.

Clean the lens with a mild solution of soapy water and a paintbrush – this really gets into the tricky areas.

The exterior of plastic lenses can be compounded with 'finnesse it' or similar fine abrasive. Do not use harsh solvents on plastic lenses as this may cause damage.

Trims or bezels can also be cleaned with soapy water, and may benefit from a polish. Even fairly grotty chrome can be transformed with a little TLC.

Seals and gaskets might be improved with a wash, or in some cases can be saved by the application of a coat of polyurethane bonding sealer. This will coat and permeate the old material, giving it new life.

Three typical rear lamp units.

VW lamp on pod.

Remove the lens and gasket.

Remove the metal reflector: note the lamp holders.

Mk2 Escort lamp.

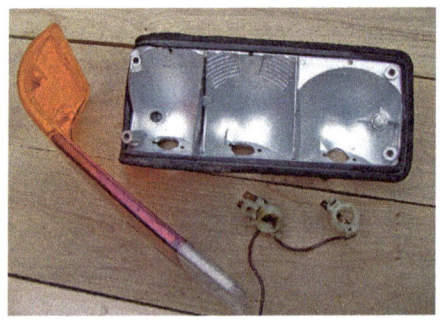

Lens removed to show plastic reflector and lamp holder.

This Triumph Herald unit shows the steel backing plate and aluminium reflectors.

Wire emerges through the foam gasket. Note the earth lead on stud.

Note – this is a very messy substance to work with though, and when it sticks, it sticks!

In the worst cases you can obtain rubber casting kits from specialist suppliers such as Frost.

Bulb holders and contacts are initially best cleaned with a paintbrush and a little WD or similar. Stubborn corrosion can be removed with wire-wool or abrasive paper.

LIGHTS AND THE LAW

Obviously, laws will vary from country to country, so I can only state what I know to be true of Britain. You would do well to consult your local vehicles inspectorate or police.

In general as laws and regulations are brought in and changed, they will apply to vehicles made after that date. As such, motors from the eighties will all show a high intensity fog lamp and a reversing light at the rear, while earlier cars are not obliged to fit them retrospectively.

Having said that, if you do decide to fit upgrades, then these must meet the appropriate standards. High-powered modern lamps fed through tired wiring is not a good idea, and fog/driving lamps should not be allowed to dazzle or confuse other road users.

Never display a white light at the

LIGHTING

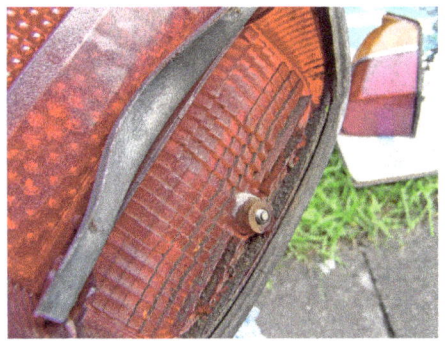

The inside of this lens has the usual grime.

Warm soapy water is used to clean inside ...

... and outside of the lamp unit.

A little fine polishing compound can ...

... transform a tired lamp ...

... and it should be a tad brighter.

rear of a vehicle. Reversing lights are to be shown only whilst travelling backward. Likewise, never display a red light at the front of a vehicle.

Blue lights are the preserve of the emergency services, and, as such, a blue light shown anywhere may constitute an offence, though many a boy-racer would not agree!

Amber or orange lights are used for indicating direction changes, though amber 'running lights', which are standard on many North American models, are usually tolerated.

Direction indicators or trafficators

Flashing amber indicators have been the norm in Britain for some years, before this semaphore type 'trafficators' were often fitted.

The 'flashing' is provided by a flasher-unit, a sealed canister which is usually found under the dashboard. The flasher is not user-serviceable and costs very little to replace.

The indicators are generally operated by means of a stalk-type switch, though a switch on the dash is not unheard of. Many German vehicles will be wired in such a way that, a sidelamp will be lit when the indicator stalk is set to one side and the ignition is off. This safety feature has led to more than a few flat batteries.

Retro fitting of a flasher system is not uncommon: details follow.

Flashing indicators look at home on this handsome Alvis.

69

ENTHUSIAST'S RESTORATION MANUAL SERIES

Additional lamps
The practice of fitting additional lamps goes back as far as motoring itself. Fog lamps – which give a low wide spread of light – or spot lamps – which have a narrow beam – have always been popular additions to older cars, even when they weren't older cars! These should complement the style of the vehicle and improve driving.

Reversing lamps are an obvious aid to manoeuvring, and some would say essential. Reversing lamps can be found which do not look out of place on most vehicles, though obviously many an enthusiast will object to any non-standard features.

In the same vein, many a car with semaphore indicators had flashers fitted, simply because they worked better, and no one thought it wrong because the cars were not held to be precious, so why be precious about it now?

Spot or fog lamps
Unless you are planning to go off-road or rallying, then the best place to fit extra lamps is on the front bumper. Lamp bars are available or you can mount them directly to the bumper blade or over-rider. You will probably need a tungsten drill bit to get through the chrome plating though.

Lamp kits are available and will supply the relevant wiring and switches along with a wiring diagram. I would be inclined to include a relay, but this is not usually essential.

If the beam from your new lamps is set in such a way that it might dazzle oncoming motorists, then you should wire it so that it is extinguished at low-beam.

Reversing lights
Reversing lamps must only be used when the vehicle is in reverse,

Huge headlights and extra lights should illuminate the road ahead.

Extra driving lamps and fog lamps on a race-ready Morgan.

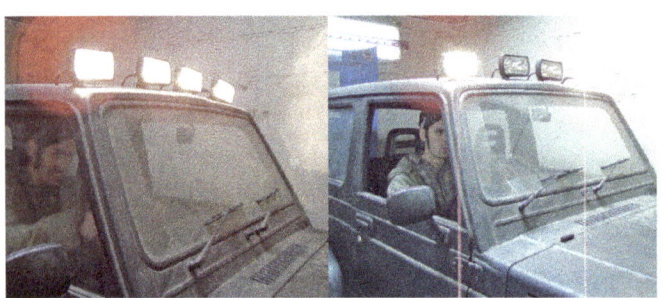

The roof-mounted lighting on my son's jeep is "mad as toast".

Retro fitted reversing lamp on this DS is discreet.

LIGHTING

An auto jumble stall at a village car show.

Genuine old bulbs can still be found.

A flasher/hazard unit, can be found in any good motor factor.

A standard Lucas flasher unit.

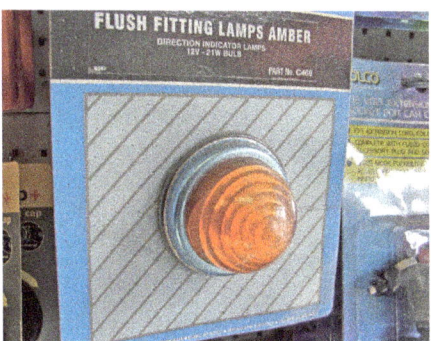

The once ubiquitous indicator lamp unit can be found on many, many vehicles.

this may sound like a pointless statement, but it is all too easy to leave the lights on if you are used to a car which cancels them automatically. To this end I would recommend a tell-tale lamp or buzzer be fitted at the same time as the lights. The necessary parts to do this can be found on the shelf of any good motor factor.

Flashing indicators

If you cannot break into the original indicator circuit, then go for a new switch of the appropriate type. Along with the lamps and switch you will also need a flasher unit and some wire. This is probably a good time to fit a hazard switch too. Again, a decent motor factor will supply a suitable 'on-off-on' switch, and if you are lucky, he can offer one featuring a hazard warning function too.

The owner of this Traction Avante tells me that the original semaphore indicators were invisible in traffic.

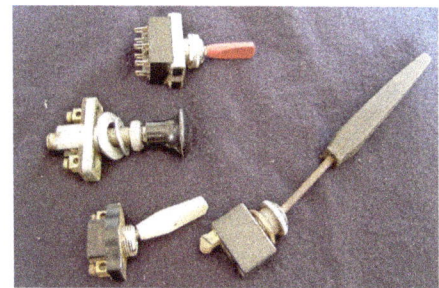

A range of old switches found at an auto jumble.

Old-fashioned bullet-nosed lamps are ideal for use as retro-fit indicators, given that that was their job for many a year.

Chapter 14
Accessories

Accessories, ancillaries, or auxiliaries – whatever you call them, the items which are not essential to the running of the engine are dealt with here.

As I have said earlier, what we think of as essential has altered considerably with the passage of time. Thirty years ago a simple radio was an expensive extra, while today my daughter reckons she couldn't do without the powered hood of her Golf cabrio!

ESSENTIAL ACCESSORIES
The horn

In legal terms, the horn is an 'audible warning device'. All electric horns operate by means of a vibrating diapragm. The diaphragm is caused to move by means of an iron 'armature' and a magnetic coil, which is fitted in close proximity to it. When the coil is energised, it draws the armature towards it, in doing so the armature opens a set of electrical contacts which in turn cut the power to the coil.

As the coil is no longer magnetic, the diaphragm, which is sprung, return to its starting position. This then closes the contacts and the cycle repeats, until the button is no longer pressed.

The exact tone or note of the horn, is governed by its number of cycles per second, the range of the armature movement, and the overall dimensions of the diaphragm. An adjuster screw, is usually to be found on the horn, this will limit the movement of the armature, and so alter the note. The addition of a trumpet will also

A standard horn as found on millions of cars.

Older horn unit.

ACCESSORIES

Air horns and pump.

The horn push is traditionally sited in the wheel boss.

Alternative horn push on dash.

modify the note, and may produce a more musical note.

Vehicles are often fitted with a pair of horns, one will be 'Low' and the other 'High' tone. Between them they should harmonise to give a pleasing sound.

When replacing a horn be certain to use the correct type.

Air horns work in the same way as electrical horns except that the diaphragm is caused to move by air which is supplied from a compressor, pump or, more rarely, an aerosol can.

Musical air-horns, are mercifully no longer tolerated on British roads. Gone are the days of that souped-up Cortina which terrorised my neighbourhood by blasting *Dixie*, at all hours!

Horn switches are traditionally mounted on the central boss of the steering wheel, the common alternative is to fit it to the base of a stalk. Switches rarely give trouble and can be tricky to repair when they do. Springs and brass contacts will, of course, fail with age and repeated use. Access to the boss is by 'popping' the horn button, from its mount.

If all else fails, a push switch can be fitted to the dash as an alternative. The power to the horn may run through a fuse and or a relay. In case of trouble check the fuse and look for power to the horn itself. The most common cause of horn failure is simply a corroded or dirty earth connection.

The windscreen wipers

The wipers are moved by a small electric motor, which will be fairly robust and simple. Over the years, though, the mechanical linkages and controls which work with the motor have evolved in ever more complex ways. Relays and timer switches are now used to govern delays, and self-parking. Earlier models will be refreshingly simple by comparison.

Failure of the wipers is commonly due to poor contacts, which may be at the earth or one of the wire terminals. Motor brushes rarely fail, though as with any older machine this is a possibility. Mechanical linkages are prone to 'gumming up', of the ancient grease, and if the motor is 'stalled' by ice or other mechanical sticking, then it may overheat. Later models will be protected by some sort of thermal overload cut-out switch.

In the event of wiper failure, you should look to the mechanicals first, followed by the wiring and relay (if fitted), before taking the motor to bits.

For fitment of electric washer pump, see below.

Heater fan

The heater fan is turned by a simple electric motor, which is very long lived and reliable in operation. As the heater draws air from outside of the vehicle it is often prone to

Typical heater motor and fan.

damp and, in some cases, water ingress. Any breach of the heater matrix may also result in water being present near the motor windings. Leaves and other debris are also a common cause of heater fan failure.

Earlier cars may have the motor encased in a steel box, which could be attached to the bulkhead on one or, possibly, both sides.

Access to the heater fan is often hampered by its placement under or behind the dashboard, and as heater systems have evolved, so the number and complexity of ducts has increased.

Steel heater-boxes are often sealed

Typical wiper motor and drive, seen here on a '60s Triumph.

A similar unit on a bench. Opening it reveals ...

... the secrets of ancient grease! This 'glue' will usually cause problems before the motor does.

ENTHUSIAST'S RESTORATION MANUAL SERIES

with a bead of mastic, and are terrible rust-traps; after cleaning and repair, a good coat of smooth Hammerite wouldn't go amiss.

Through the seventies, moulded plastic boxes became the norm, these, of course, do not rust, but are often not designed to be dismantled or serviced.

NON-ESSENTIAL ACCESSORIES

Dependent on the age of your vehicle, you may find an unused 'accessory' fuse which is designed to be employed when fitting extras. If no capacity is available on the existing fuse board you may run a line directly from the battery terminal to the new device. This must, of course, include an appropriate fuse.

If you intend to fit more than one ancillary device, then the option of a second fuse board is a good one. Take a wire of an appropriate gauge from the positive battery terminal and then take feeds to the new goodies which can all be covered by fuses of the correct size.

Radio

A correct period radio is something that really gives credibility to an older car. Conversely, few things look so wrong as a modern radio in a classic dashboard. Genuine old radios are available from garage sales and on the Internet, while

The underside of the unit shows dual polarity. Ensure correct setting.

Genuine '60s push button radio found in a box of junk.

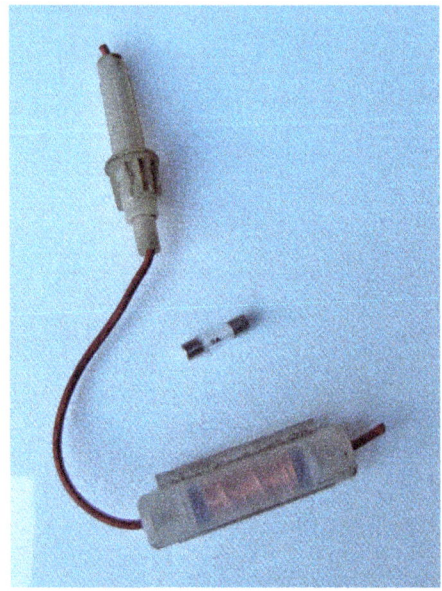

The radio wiring harness has an inline fuse and line choke to smooth out the current.

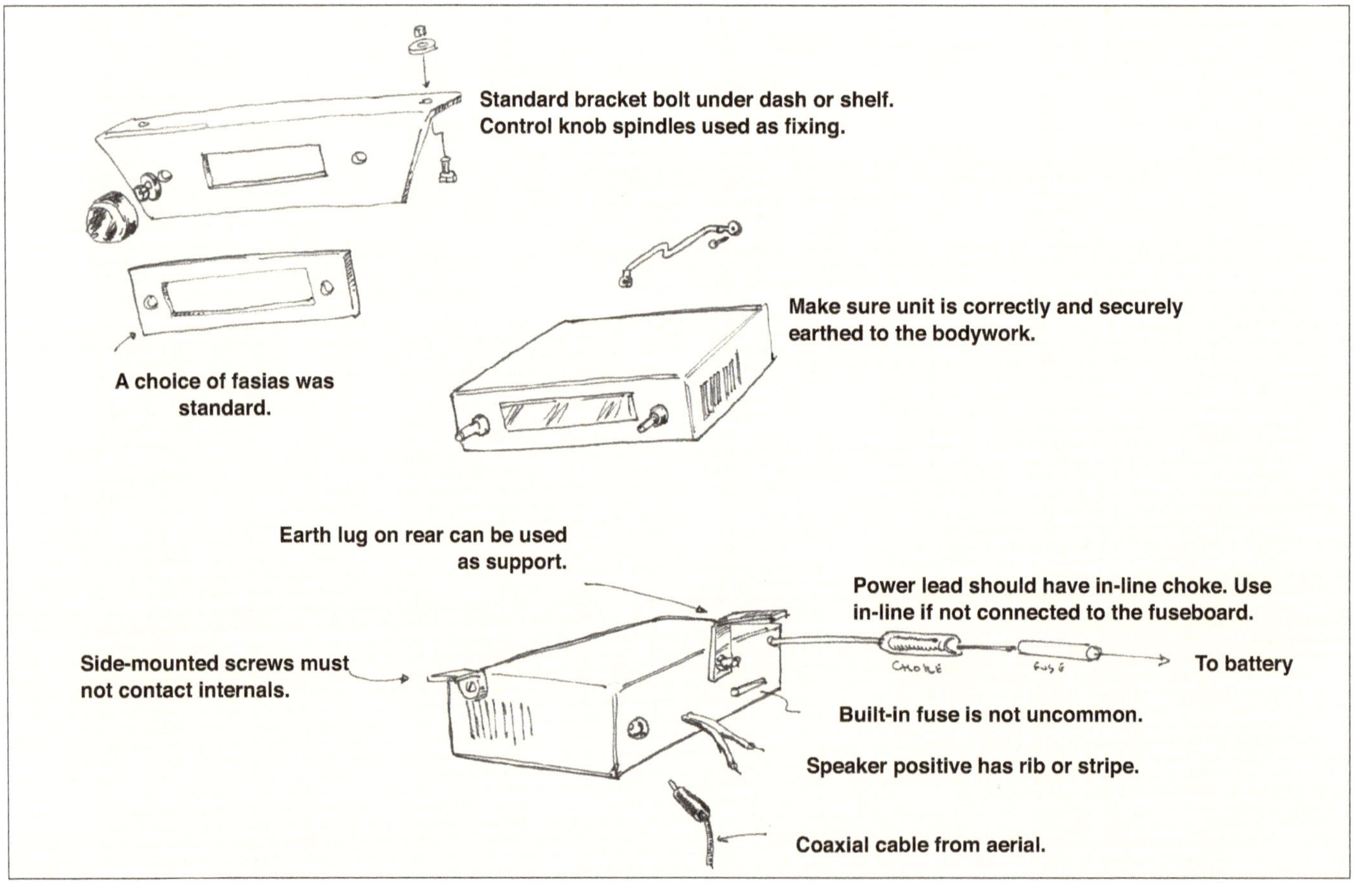

Standard bracket bolt under dash or shelf. Control knob spindles used as fixing.

A choice of fasias was standard.

Make sure unit is correctly and securely earthed to the bodywork.

Earth lug on rear can be used as support.

Side-mounted screws must not contact internals.

Power lead should have in-line choke. Use in-line if not connected to the fuseboard.

To battery

Built-in fuse is not uncommon.

Speaker positive has rib or stripe.

Coaxial cable from aerial.

ACCESSORIES

The stylish dash and interior do not benefit from a modern radio.

panel beaters and mechanics are notorious hoarders of old radios.

Be certain to fit one of the correct polarity, and if the thing is of unknown provenance you should have it checked out by a qualified electrician before chancing it in your beloved motor.

Mounting brackets are fairly standard, though the manufacturer of your particular vehicle may well have produced a bespoke one. If so, then that one will always be preferable, but may be a little tricky to find.

Fitting a negative earth radio to a positive earth vehicle is possible, but the whole thing must be isolated, and not allowed to earth through its casing.

Some sixties units, like the one shown here, feature dual polarity. Make sure that yours is set correctly.

You can, of course, hide a decent modern unit in the glove box – the older units might look better but they won't work nearly as well. Specialist companies can supply modern radios built into old casings – very tasty! Check out Vintage Wireless Co.

Connect the radio to the accessory fuse if one is fitted; alternatively, you can wire it directly to the battery. Fit an in-line fuse as well as a line-choke, to smooth out the current.

Never use the vehicle body to return the speaker signal, instead use proper speaker cable, which will feature a rib or line to denote the positive wire, which will carry the signal to the speaker. Do not be conned into buying overpriced hi-fi cable, as it will not make your '60s Motorola sound any better!

Capacitors can be fitted to any electrical device, which might give off stray emissions, this prevents interference to your radio.

Note – a radio or any other device which is not covered by the key switch, may flatten your battery if used for extended periods without the engine running.

Electric washer pump

Cute as it is to have a rubber bulb to squirt water at our windscreen, there are times when it might not keep up with the road-spray coming off that lorry on the M40.

A washer pump will cost just a few quid and can be discretely fitted to most cars. Motorised pumps can be found which sit in line with the water pipes and so do not require any alteration to the reservoir or jets.

At worst you can fit a modern reservoir with a motorised pump built in to it. It need not be permanent and so need not detract from your car's originality.

Heated rear window

This is another item many of us would now take for granted with a

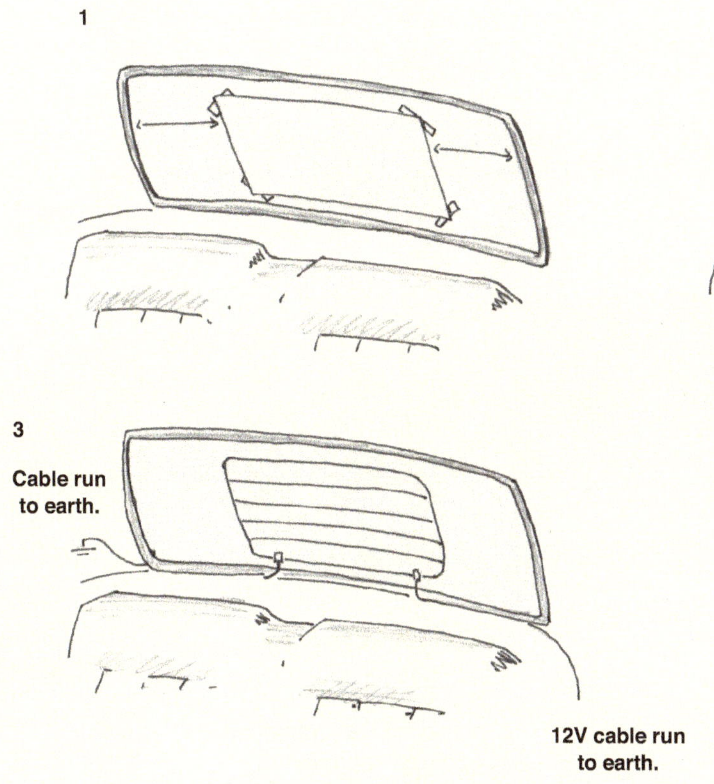

1

2

3 Cable run to earth.

12V cable run to earth.

1 Fix paper to outside of rear window.

2 Fix heated section to inside of screen over template.

3 Connect one terminal to a good earth. Run live feed along sill under carpet and up to suitable fused switch.

ENTHUSIAST'S RESTORATION MANUAL SERIES

A battery key switch is a neat means of immobilising the vehicle.

Or you could simply fit a discrete switch inline with your coil.

newer car, but one which actually became standard as late as the early eighties. Some luxury models featured heated front screens much earlier, these are now rather valuable and rare.

The true heated rear screen or de-mister is made up of a series of fine wires embedded in the glass. The wire does not get 'hot' so much, as raise the temperature enough to prevent frost and condensation.

Crude early screens which have the elements printed or glued to the glass can be repaired with a conductive material. This is painted on with a brush and is available from Frosts and other good suppliers

On a cold morning it would be wise to deploy such a device only after the engine has been started, as they do draw quite a bit of power.

Retro fit plastic heated rear screens which many of us will be familiar with are still available and do work pretty well. A better alternative is the retro fit heater, which is transferred onto the screen. These are a tad trickier to fit, but neater and more effective.

If you choose to fit one, be certain to use a switch with a tell-tale light as you don't want to be wasting power running the thing, when its not needed.

As with the radio, wire the heated screen to the accessory fuse if one is fitted or take the feed directly from the battery with a suitable in-line fuse.

Electric windows

Electric windows began to appear on mass-produced vehicles in the mid-seventies, but even as late as the mid-eighties, it was not uncommon to find an emergency winding handle just in case. I'm thinking of the Lancia Beta here, and I won't comment further.

Just as with manual window winders, motor manufacturers have tried endless variations of the lift mechanism. Some feature a pantograph arm while others utilise cables and pulleys.

Pantograph type lever arms will usually be paired with a coil spring to counter the weight of the glass. The actual motor will generally be of the shunt-wound or permanent magnet variety, and will be very dependable in normal use.

Problems with a window lifter are, therefore, more than likely down to mechanical problems with the linkage or runners. Dirt in the gears is not uncommon, and in some cases worn teeth on a drive sprocket will be found.

I would always be inclined to clean up and grease the entire linkage, rather than dismantle a window motor. Basic electrical checks to establish continuity would, of course, be prudent.

Alarms and immobilisers

The simplest way to immobilise your vehicle is to disconnect the wire to the coil LT. A discrete toggle switch on the dash (or tucked away beneath it) will prevent the engine from firing.

A huge range of alarms and immobilisation gear is available, and all will come with comprehensive fitting instructions.

If you do buy and fit an alarm, don't be seduced by remote controls and the like. My first hi-tech security device consisted of an LED and a 22k ohm resistor, these were fitted into a small box which sat on the dash. I knew it was just a light, but no one else did!

Most security systems will need a fused power supply, plus a feed from the courtesy lamp circuit (to tell it when the door is opened.) Be prepared to fit a couple of new plunger switches and mount a motion sensor. Or you could go for self-contained unit which simply sits in the car.

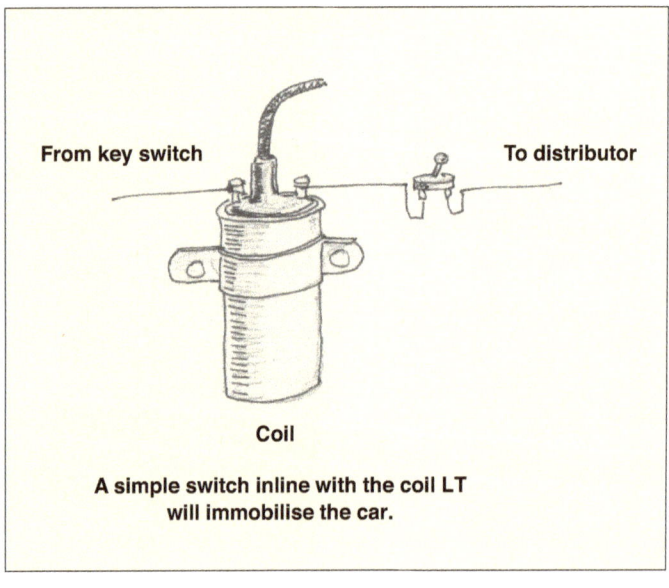

A simple switch inline with the coil LT will immobilise the car.

Chapter 15
Instrumentation

Thirty-five or forty years ago, the only instrument required by law was the speedo, all the rest were either for driver convenience or, in many cases, just for show. Then again, in those days a simple clock was considered a luxury.

The various dials and gauges that you might find on a classic automobile where designed to last the life of the vehicle, which was reckoned to be about ten years or one-hundred thousand miles. Your instruments were never meant to be serviceable, and this fact is reflected in the way that they are put together.

Specialist instrument restorers and calibrators can be found through owners clubs and on the Internet. We, as enthusiasts, are more realistically limited to cleaning and polishing our dials. Having said that, it is worth knowing how your car's dials work; I have rescued a few with just a light touch from a fine paintbrush. Also, by simply removing and cleaning the cover glass and bezel you can appear to work wonders.

THE SPEEDOMETER

The speedometer is the most important dial in many respects, however, other than its backlight (if one is fitted), the speedo is not actually part of the electrical system.

The speedometer is driven by a rotating cable, which is in turn driven by the car's gearbox. Where the cable meets the speedometer it turns a magnet inside a metal drum. As the magnet spins it attracts the drum and causes it to turn in sympathy. Attached to the drum are the speedometer needle and a return

The dashboard sets the tone of your car.

77

ENTHUSIAST'S RESTORATION MANUAL SERIES

A standard speedometer unit is found in many less exotic machines.

Rev counter may be mechanical or electronic.

Drum is attached to pointer.

Magnet is turned by gearbox.

Speedometer is mechanically driven.

spring. Thus the faster the magnet spins, so the harder it draws the drum and the further across the gauge the needle swings.

Variations on the needle are all based on the same principle, cloth or paper rolls may be used to give the impression of a moving line on a horizontal graph.

The commonest fault with speedometers is due to a worn cable; before the cable gives out, it may cause a 'chacka, chacka' sound or a rhythmic jumping of the needle. This might be cured or improved by the application of a little light oil. Some models will feature a lubrication point for this purpose.

MILEOMETER/ODOMETER

This is linked to the speedo and is driven by the same rotating cable. The milometer or odometer is a simple mechanical counter. Manually adjusting the mileage is usually termed as 'clocking' the car and is frowned upon. If you have overhauled the engine then re-setting the mileage to zero is OK, but obviously will not reflect the true life of the car. Fitting a new speedometer is considered as 'kosher' but can give rise to ambiguity.

Mileage counters rarely need work other than cleaning.

TACHOMETER OR REV COUNTER

The rev counter was, for many years, the preserve of the high-performance or luxury car.

The dial may be mechanically driven in the same manner as the speedo, but more likely it will be electrical, with the sender being linked to the contact-breaker. This type relies on converting the pulses generated by the opening of the points into a voltage which can measured by the dial. The dial will, therefore, be based on a moving iron (magnet), moving coil, or bimetallic strip (see diagrams).

TEMPERATURE GAUGE

The water temperature gauge works on the principle of variable resistance within a sensor which is attached to the engine in close proximity to one of the waterways. A stable voltage is passed to the dial and on to the sensor. As the water heats up, so the resistance alters and this is registered by the dial, the needle of which is supported by a bimetallic strip. As the voltage rises the strip is heated and deforms to produce movement.

Moving coil

Moving coil dials are rather like a very light-duty DC motor in which the armature can only rotate about 90°. The needle/armature is mounted on two spiral springs which are set in such a way as to negate any thermal interference. The springs are also the contacts for the armature current. This type of dial is rather complicated and delicate, it is also sensitive to movement. Look at an old voltmeter.

Moving iron

Moving iron (moving magnet) dials utilise the relative attraction of two magnets on an iron armature which is attached to a needle. One of the attracting magnets has a constant voltage while the other will have a voltage which is varied according to the sender unit.
This type of unit is un-damped and so is a bit prone to bouncing around.

INSTRUMENTATION

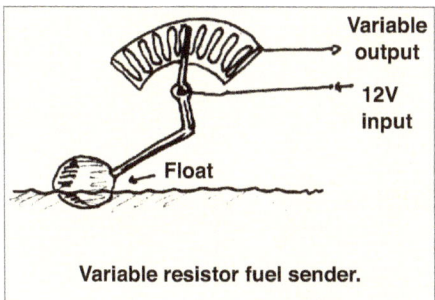

Variable resistor fuel sender.

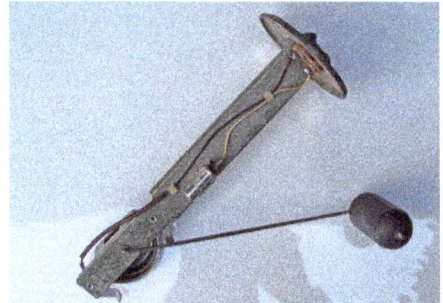

The fuel sender unit consists of a float connected to a variable resistor.

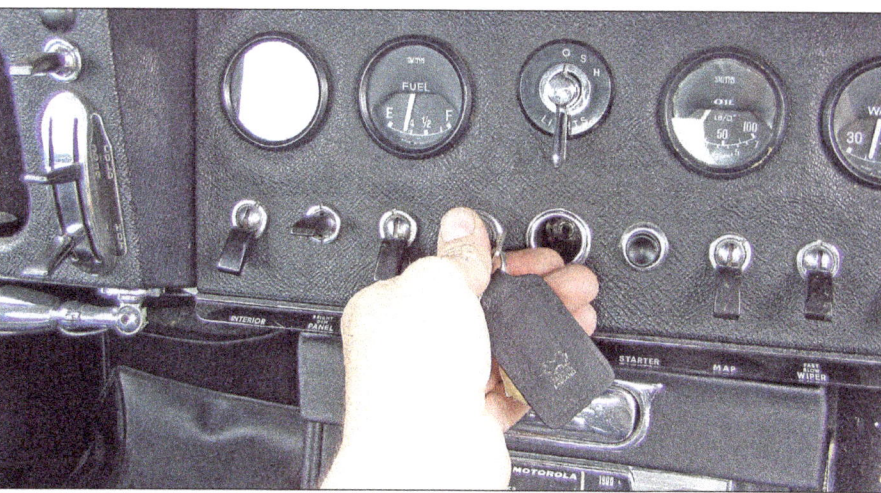

A fuel gauge is essential on a dashboard.

PETROL GAUGE

The petrol gauge is operated by variable resistance, in a similar method to the temperature gauge.

A bimetallic strip causes the gauge needle to move as the voltage within the sender unit alters.

The sender unit is mounted within the petrol tank, and consists of a float which is attached via a lever to a coil which acts as a variable resistor. As the float rises and falls, so the amount of resistor which is in circuit alters, thus relaying the position of the fuel level to the instrument panel.

Damp within the tank can lead to corrosion and poor conduction of the contacts. Servicing of the sender is not out of the question, but extreme care must be taken should you choose to get involved with anything that requires electricity and petrol vapours to be brought together.

AMMETER

The ammeter or amp-meter is a handy thing on an older car, as it keeps the driver in touch with the state of the charging system. If not fitted as standard, then an aftermarket unit is worth the trouble to fit.

The meter is placed in circuit with the generator, and measures the current as it flows based on the magnetic field which is produce by that flow.

OIL PRESSURE GAUGE

The oil pressure gauge may be electrical or mechanical.

Mechanical type

The mechanical oil pressure gauge is fed

An ammeter is a useful device on an older vehicle.

with engine oil via a fine pipe. Within the gauge the needle is attached to a flexible tube which, when pressurised, deforms to cause movement.

While this type of dial can be an accurate measure of the oil pressure, and in some respects a good indication of the state of the engine, the obvious drawback with this set-up, is that failure can be very messy.

Electrical type

Electrical oil pressure gauges are similar to the petrol or temperature gauge seen above, but the sender is mounted in an

Two oil gauges – they look similar ...

A retro fit ammeter is easily fitted.

oil-way and translates pressure against a spring-loaded resistor into a voltage.

A common and cheaper alternative to an oil gauge is a simple oil pressure light. In such a set up the light is triggered by a sprung switch, which is mounted in an oil-way.

When the ignition is turned on, the oil warning lamp on the dash will be lit, as no pressure is available to overcome the spring and the switch contacts will be closed.

... but the rear view shows that the one on the left is pressure fed.

79

ENTHUSIAST'S RESTORATION MANUAL SERIES

CLOCK

The earliest clocks to be found in an automobile where actually clockwork. Electric clocks are exactly what you might expect them to be – 12V electric clocks. As such, if you wouldn't try to mend the one in your front room, then you probably wont get too far mending the one in your car.

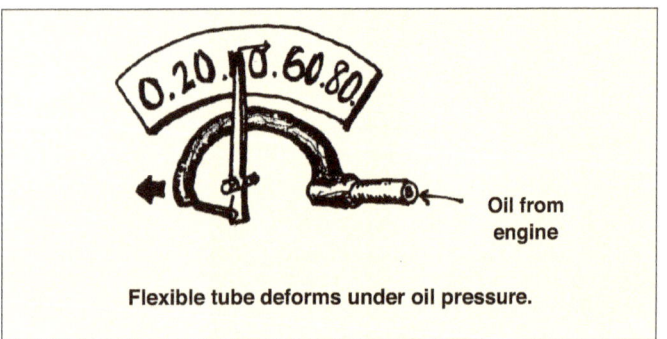

Flexible tube deforms under oil pressure.

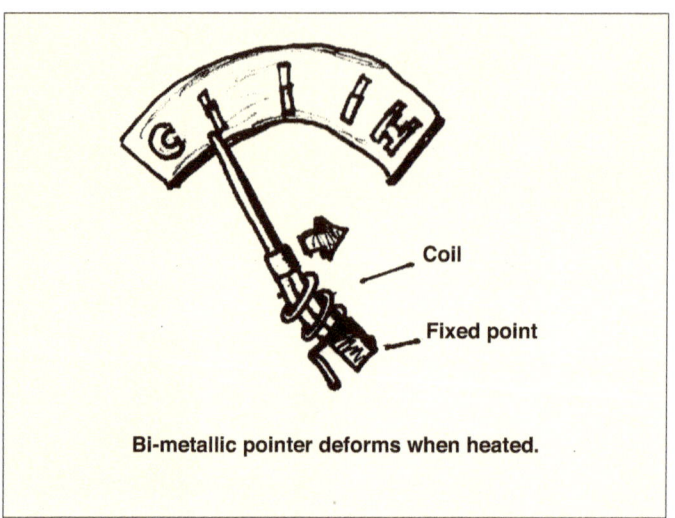

Bi-metallic pointer deforms when heated.

The dial is looking rather sad.

The rear shows clamp and connections.

Dial in bits; remove dust with a paint brush.

Back in one piece – that's much better.

Chapter 16
Wires, fuses & switches

Wires, fuses, switches, and connectors – all the stuff which go to make up the wiring harness or loom. There is no point in looking at the major components, if we pay no heed to the pathway of the current that feeds them.

Many of the problems that hamper the older vehicle are caused by simple things such as a loose spade, a broken wire or by furring up of a connector. We need to understand and maintain our wiring if we are going to keep our classics on the road.

WIRING
The loom/harness

The wires that connect your vehicle's various components together are collectively known as its 'loom' or 'harness'.

Traditionally the wires are bundled together and bound with a non-adhesive tape; on earlier models this binding would be of cotton, and on later cars of PVC plastic. The ends and junctions would be sealed with an adhesive tape to prevent unravelling.

Earlier and simpler vehicles will tend to have fewer wires and the loom will often be in one piece, as the automobile has evolved to ever more complex specifications, so the loom has grown with it. Later and more sophisticated cars will probably have a loom made up of several pieces, and while more joints does mean more potential corrosion, it also means less chance that someone has chopped it up while replacing a wing.

The majority of our classics will have a fuse board mounted on, or through, the bulkhead (firewall). As such, many of the wires will commonly be broken at this point.

When replacing an entire wiring loom, it is a good idea to

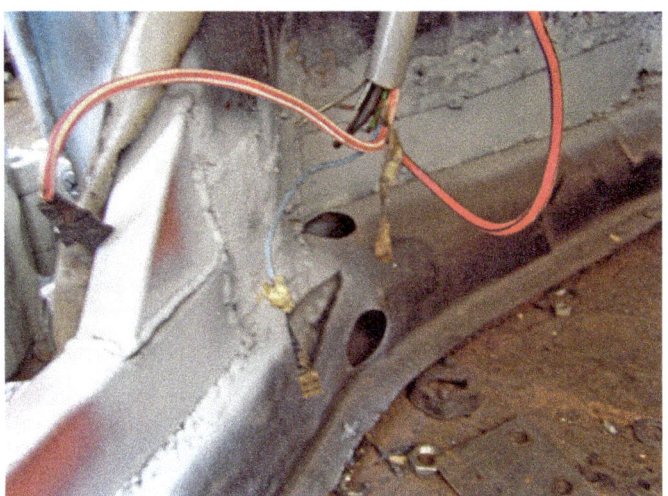

The main wiring harness should pass through the hole in the sill.

Typical wiring – untidy taped joints, but at least it is colour-coded.

use the fuse board as the point to work toward, which is to say, forward from the rear and backward from the engine bay (see below).

Wire and cables

We will most commonly find electrical wires made up of strands of copper and steel. These will be enclosed in a non-conductive coating such as PVC plastic or rubber and cotton. Earlier rubber/cotton type insulators will perish after time, and even the hardiest of sticklers for originality will usually opt to replace the old wiring with a modern substitute.

The size of each cable and the number of strands that make it up will be related to the amount of current that it will carry, so, when replacing cables or fitting new equipment, be certain to use a wire which can handle the load. Failure to do so will place your car at risk of fire or electrical damage. Bear in mind that the rating of any cable is by the metre; if you double the length, so you will double the resistance. See chart for cable rating.

Colour codes and fault tracing

Over the years manufacturers have attempted to bring in standards for colour coding, and within one company, or era, you may find some semblance of order. Overall though chaos rules. You will often find the same colour of wire used to perform several jobs around the car and some models will have a loom composed of entirely black wires ... which can make tracing any particular wire rather slow.

The original manufacturer's wiring diagram will show a colour code key, but beware of updates within the life span of your vehicle.

Stress fracturing and metal fatigue in wiring

The phenomenon of stress fracture or metal fatigue is very common in wiring. Most metals will become brittle or 'work hardened' if repeatedly bent one way and then the other; copper and steel cable are not exceptions. Failure of this sort is often to be found near to where a section of cable is rigidly fixed. In most cases the remedy is simply a matter of shortening the wire. The same is true of many household electrical appliances, and explains why we so often find a length of supporting sheath around the cable.

Connections

Ideally our loom or harness would feature no breaks or joins in the wiring, but practicality dictates that it will. The next best thing would be for all the joints to be soldered, again mass production and the risk of damage caused by heat makes this idea a non-starter.

Whatever type of connection you employ, always remember the adage: "The basis of a good electrical joint is a good mechanical joint."

Screwed or bolted cable ends

It is not uncommon to find wires and cable that terminate at a screw or bolt which connects them to the respective component. This type of joint is mechanically sound, but tends to suffer from metal fatigue, and corrosion. Bare wire connections can be improved with an appropriate 'washer type' cable end.

Push-fit connectors

As a compromise we tend to find push-fit connectors; these may be attached to their respective wires by soldering, crimping or simply held together by friction.

Most push-fit connectors will be self-cleaning, which is to say

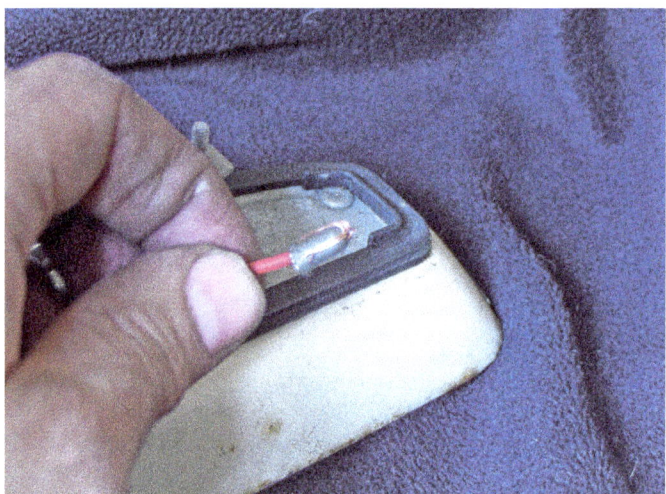

This old-fashioned bullet connector has wire passed through and turned back ...

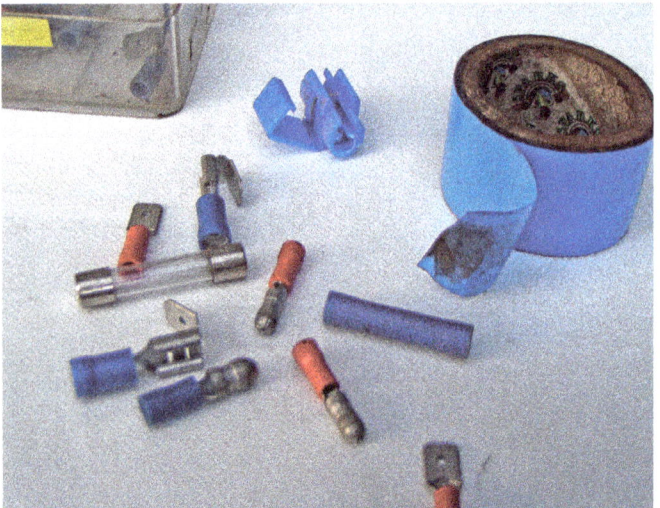

Odd connectors, insulating tape and a Scotchlok.

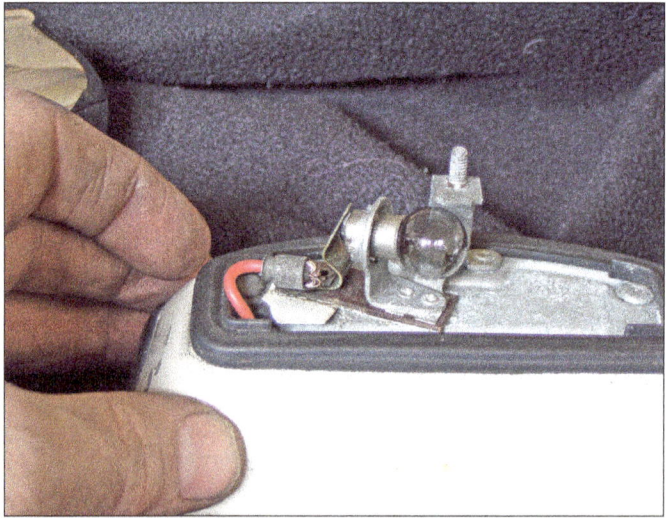

... the bullet is then pushed into its counterpart.

WIRES, FUSES & SWITCHES

The correct tool for crimping original bullet connectors – with thanks to Frost.

that by simply pulling the joint apart and then pushing it together, you will effectively strip it of any oxide build up. It will often pay you to tighten up the connector, which may involve a little pressure from a pair of pliers.

Lucar type connectors or spades are still in common use and are available from any high street hardwear or motorist shop. Most are designed to be crimped on the wire and are available in kits, which come complete with crimper and a range of connectors.

It pays to buy a half-decent crimper rather than going for the cheapest.

Ideally you can solder the wires to the Lucar connector (see below).

Bullet type connectors were often originally designed in such a way that the wires would have been passed through the nose of the connector and turned back over. By then pushing the male bullet into its female counterpart, the wires are trapped and against the sleeve to make the contact.

The modern take on the bullet is also shown here and can be crimped or soldered.

Scotchlok

The 3M Scotchlok was introduced in the late seventies, and was heralded as the great instant wire connector. Many professionals dearly hate the things and I would advise that they only be used as a purely temporary fixing (for which they are brilliant).

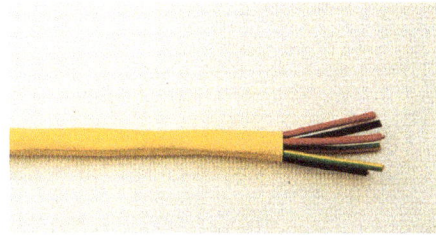

Just heat to shrink – shrink wrap is a very popular product.

Shrink wrap

Shrink wrap is a handy method of sealing and insulating an electrical joint. Though obviously not very original, Mike Wood at Frost tells me that this is one of their most popular products. The shrink wrap is placed around the newly formed joint and heated. The wrap then shrinks and forms an effective seal.

Insulating tape

Insulating tape is one of the all time great problem solvers. No tool-box is complete with at least one roll. This marvellous product can be used to wrap all manner of electrical joints and loose ends.

Soldering

However tightly a joint is crimped, the possibility of moisture ingress is ever present. The best method of joining a wire to a connector, or a wire to another wire, is to solder it.

Soldering is a simple process, but one that takes a little bit of care and know-how.

Invest in a decent soldering iron, preferably one with a stand as you will often need to put the thing down while it is hot. Gun type irons are quick to heat up and have a built-in light.

Multi-cored solder has a flux formed into it, so making the process easier.

Warning! – Solder fumes are hazardous.

How to solder a connector to a wire

There are two schools of thought here: one says to 'tin' the wire first, and the other says to heat both parts at once.

Method 1. 'Tinning' the wire

1. Heat the iron and have it to hand. A stand is handy here.
2. Strip away an appropriate length of insulation from the wire.
3. Use the iron to heat the exposed wire until it is hot enough to melt the solder on contact.
4. Continue applying heat while feeding the solder into the wire until it is fully permeated.
5. Remove the heat and allow solder to cool.
6. Fit connector in place and close if possible.
7. Re-heat with the iron until solder flows onto the connector.
8. Allow to cool.
9. In some case you may 'tin' both parts to be joined. This method ensures that the solder has bonded to each part and is not simply sitting on one – a situation known as a 'dry' joint.

Method 2. Heating both parts together

1. Heat the iron and have it to hand. A stand is handy here.

Soldering iron on home-made stand.

ENTHUSIAST'S RESTORATION MANUAL SERIES

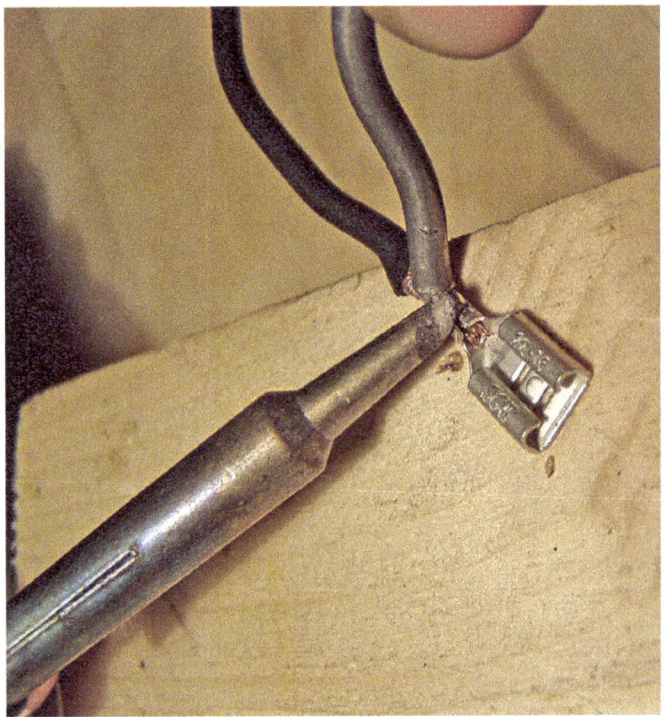

Solder is applied to heated wire and connector.

Earthing points
The practice of using the vehicle's body to return the current to the battery demands that some wires will need to be 'earthed' or terminated directly to the metalwork. In order to improve conductivity, such earth points often feature a toothed washer. Rust and corrosion are common problems in and around these areas.

Two earth leads looking for a bolt to run the power to the bodywork.

2. Strip away an appropriate length of insulation from the wire.
3. Put the wire and the connector together as they should be, and close if possible.
4. Press the tip of the soldering iron firmly to the connector at the joint. Try not to touch the wire itself as the idea is to heat the connector first, this is because the copper of the wire is more 'heat conductive' than the steel connector. With the two pieces held together, the wire should absorb enough heat as is. The key to getting a good soldered joint is to heat both pieces equally.
5. Feed a little solder into the joint, if the heat is right it should melt on contact and flow nicely onto the surfaces of both pieces.
6. Once you are happy with the flow of the solder remove the iron and let the solder cool and harden.

You may now wish to use shrink-wrap or insulating tape to seal the end of the wire onto the spade.

If you've never soldered a joint before, I'd advise practising on a few unwanted pieces first. A common fault with first timers is to use too much solder, thus making an untidy bulky joint or to only heat one piece, causing a weak joint (dry joint).

If the solder forms a bubble on one of the pieces, then the heat hasn't flowed between the two pieces evenly. The more the heat spreads around the heated area the more the solder will flow, try not to let the pieces get so hot as to let this happen too much. The solder should appear to 'cling' to both pieces, and should stay fairly localised. A slight roundness is ok, but never a bead, as this would suggest that the solder has melted, but is not actually bonding. And, with practice it's easy to tell a good joint from a bad one. Look for a smooth shiny appearance.

Be aware, also, that too much heat may damage components, and if the parts to be soldered are oxidised, you should use a flux such as Bakers Fluid or any powdered flux mixed with a little water.

Note – all fluxes and solders will tend to be highly toxic, as are their fumes. Handle with care and only solder in a well-ventilated area.

Untidy earth point on 1960s car would benefit from a clean.

FUSES
Fuses, fusible links and contact-breakers, are essentially 'weak links' in a circuit. The idea is to protect our components by causing the power supply to fail if the current is excessive.

In its most basic form, the fuse is a short length of wire between two terminals. Ceramic fuses are common on earlier motors, while glass tube and blade fuses are normal on our classics. You may also find heavy-duty fuses known as 'fusible links' or 'circuit-breakers' sited away from the board, possibly in the engine bay. These protect the whole system, and may not be mentioned in the handbook.

WIRES, FUSES & SWITCHES

A selection of fuse types.

A new fuse board is a good idea when fitting electrical extras.

A seriously large fuse board in a new American monster.

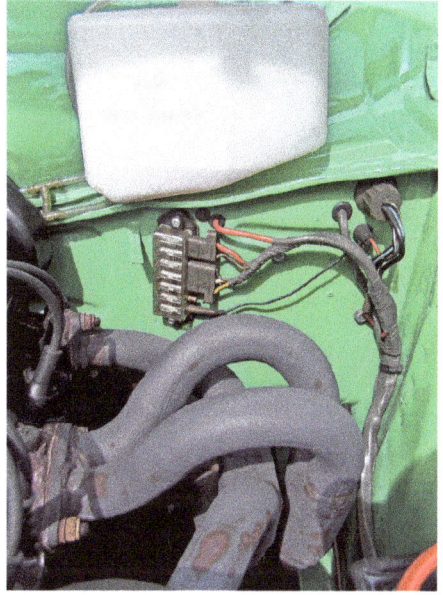
A nice tidy fuse board on a Mk1 Escort.

This 1957 Riley has a modern fuse board to go with its updated electrics.

As the motor car has evolved, so the demands on the electrical system have grown dramatically. A typical vehicle of the sixties might have featured three, four or five fuses, including a spare for optional accessories such as a radio. Just a few years later, in mid-seventies vehicles, we will find a fuse board featuring a dozen or more fuses.

When updating or adding to your electrical system, you will need to fit more fuses; these can be individual – as in the in-line type, or mounted as a second fuse board.

Working with and around the loom

Many mechanical and bodywork jobs will inevitably bring you into contact with your vehicle's wiring. Changing a wing or repairing a rear quarter panel will demand that wires be disconnected or moved to safety. It is all too easy to forget when cutting into a panel that an electrical supply may be hidden behind it. The golden rule is to check first, clear everything safely out of the way, and, most importantly, label everything. This might sound unnecessary, but believe me: connections which appear really obvious when dismantling your car, often become rather obtuse when putting it back together. A simple flag of tape will normally suffice in the short term, but any writing will fade with time. And, as many of us are a little bit optimistic when it come to the time scale of our projects ...

My favoured method of flagging is to tape any wires from one component together with a flag naming that item, I then place a dot of paint onto each individual cable, and onto its corresponding connection on the component itself. This may be long-winded but it sure works. If the connections to a particular item are of differing size of shape then this become a whole lot easier.

Replacing a front wing

In order to replace a front wing you will typically have to remove a headlamp, an indicator, and possibly a side repeater lamp. The wires which feed these lamps will most likely pass from the engine bay through the flitch plate (inner wing) via a grommet into the front wheel area where they will be covered with muddy water. The headlamp wires will usually pass via another grommet into the backing bowl of the headlamp.

85

ENTHUSIAST'S RESTORATION MANUAL SERIES

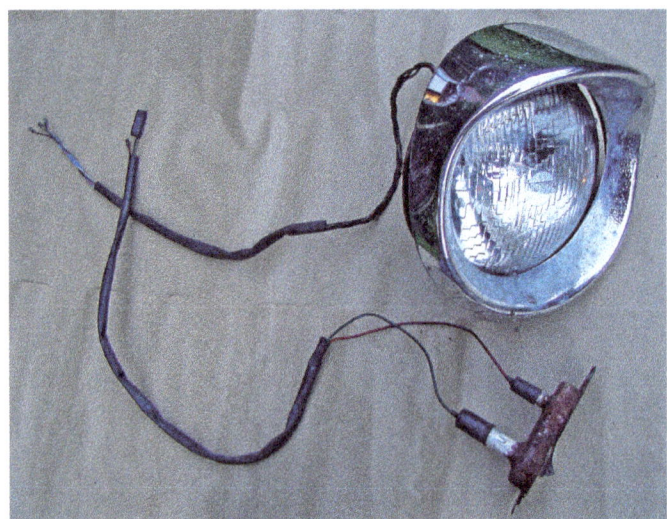

Typical wiring that will be encountered when replacing a front wing.

It is tempting, when removing a panel, to think of the lamp wires as a minor detail which can be ignored or left until the wing has been unbolted or cut off. Many is the time that I have seen a wing hanging by its lamp cables. The great temptation at this point is to cut the wires and have done with it. This is all well and good, and indeed in some cases quite proper, but, often as not, a cursory glance will reveal the wires to be broken just inside the engine bay or simply plugged into the lamp unit. By supporting the weight of the panel on the wire, you are quite likely to cause damage which may not reveal itself for some time.

It pays to take the time to undo the electrics before attacking the panel itself, and if you must cut a wire think about how you will repair it first. Once disconnected, all wiring should be coiled up, flagged where appropriate, and stashed out of harm's way.

Typical RQP or mid-panel repair

Many of your car's panels will conceal wiring, and it is all too easy to get carried away with a cutting disk or chisel before realising that you have just destroyed the supply to the rear lights. Enthusiasm

When cutting into a rear quarter panel, it is all too easy to forget the wiring concealed within.

is a great thing when it comes to restoration, but patience is truly a virtue. Before you get stuck-in, take the time to move any wiring well out of the way using tape or cable ties. Better still, disconnect the wires, flag as need be, and roll the cable back to a safe point. Again, if you must chop a wire, give thought to how it will be repaired first.

Making up a section of loom – with thanks to Mike Wood at Frost

There may be times when your best option is to replace or make a section of wiring. I have known people fabricate entire looms from scratch – it makes spaghetti look neat, so lets start with something simple. Obviously this is a whole lot easier if you have the old wires to copy.

Gather up some string, scissors, panel pins, and a board long enough to take the section to be made.
1. Begin by deciding just how much you need to make and where it will mate to the existing wiring. If a natural break can be found, then this is probably going to be simpler than joining lots of wires together with solder.
2. Lay lengths of string where the original wires would have run, or alongside the originals. Tape these together as need be and label each carefully. Different colours of string are an obvious advantage at this stage.
3. Next, transfer the string loom onto the board with panel pins at any key points. All pertinent information can also be written alongside.
4. Now systematically replace each piece of string with wire of the appropriate grade and colour. Make any joins as necessary, and tape together at any branches.
5. With the wiring in one piece, you can now attend to the terminals.
6. Now bind the wires. You will find that keeping as much of the new loom section on the board for as long as possible will keep tangles to a minimum.
7. Finally, transfer your new section of wiring into the vehicle.

Loom swap

There are three reasons why you might want to completely remove and refit the wiring harness: during a complete ground up restoration, a body swap, and in order to renew the wiring en toto. Essentially the job is the same in each case, but if the wiring is new, you have little control of how well it is labelled and, as with many wiring jobs, labelling is the key to not getting in a mess. Obviously, how complicated the task is depends on the complexity of the vehicle in question. Taking notes and photographs is a good idea, and flag all connections no matter how obvious they look. Remove the battery before anything else.

De-trim the interior of the vehicle. How much you remove will be governed by the sophistication of the electrics. For example, most domestic saloons or sports cars of the '60s or early '70s will not have any wiring to the doors, whereas later models of all types will commonly have electric window, puddle lights and speakers (the latter is more likely to be an add on and not connected to the loom). Looking at '80s machines, central locking and speaker cables will be part and parcel – whether the components are fitted to a particular car or not. As a rule the main bulk of the wiring will run through the car along one or both sills, usually in a pressed groove. From here it will most likely pass into the RQP and over the rear arch into the boot area, where it will feed the rear lights.

Minor branches to items such as the gear selector may be taped to the floor under the carpet, or may drop from under the dash centrally.

The front seats, as a rule, do not need to be removed, but their absence will make the job of removing the dash and any side trims a whole lot easier. The dash is the most difficult of jobs, if only because of the shear number of wires hiding behind it. Bear

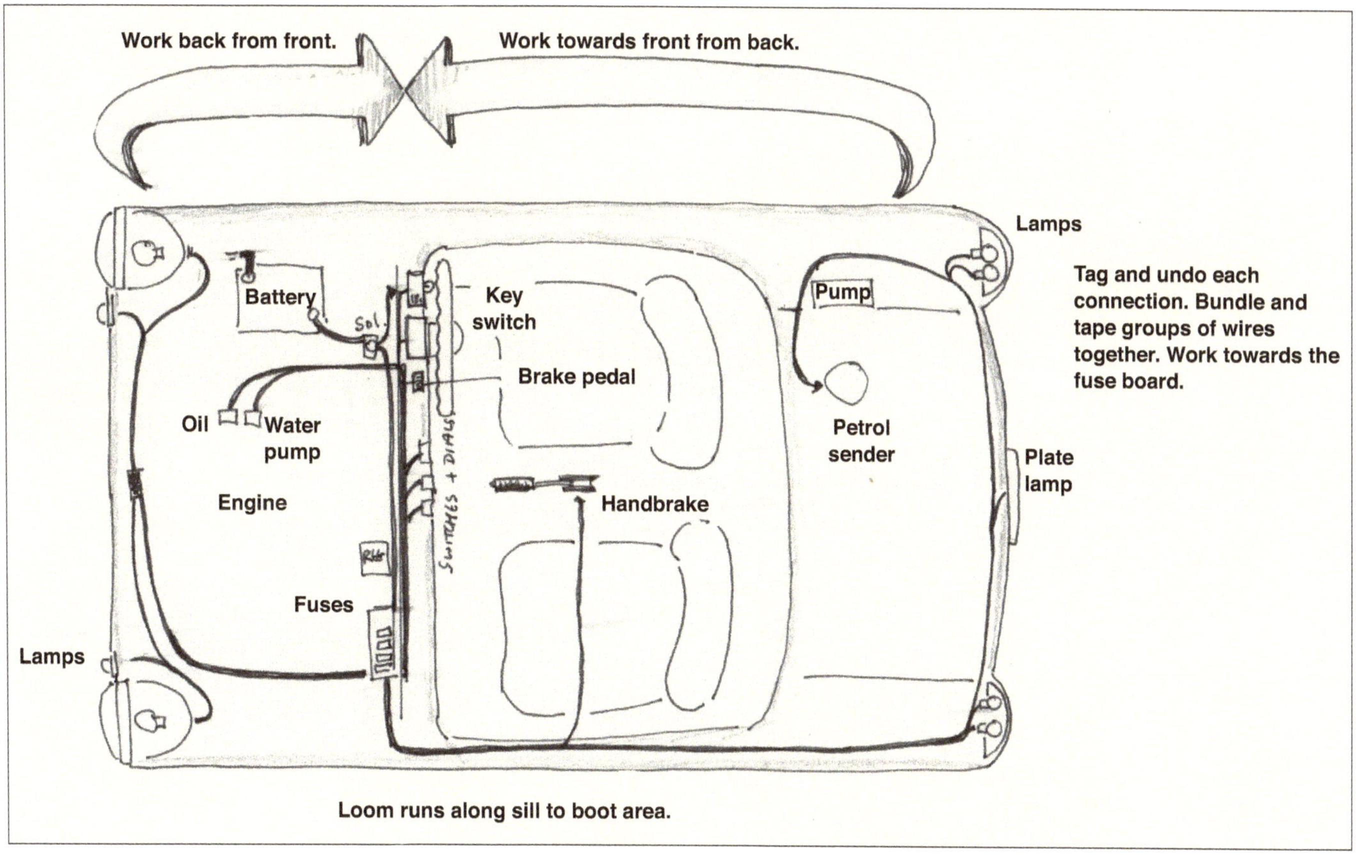

WIRES, FUSES & SWITCHES

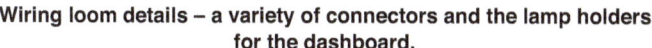

The loom swap requires a plan of action – don't just wade in!

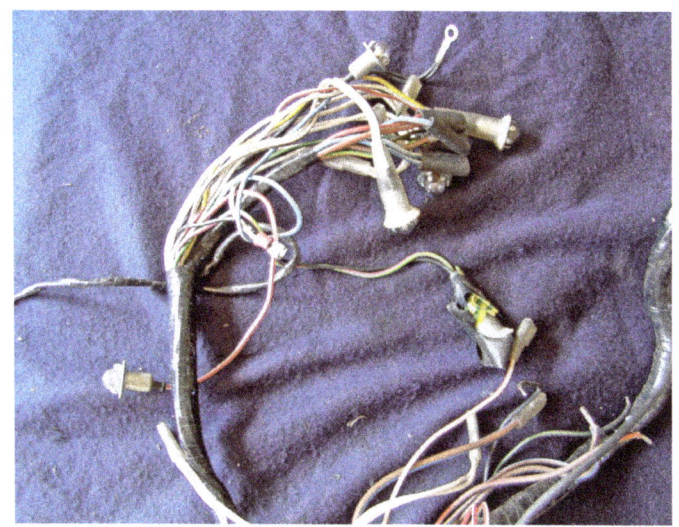

Wiring loom details – a variety of connectors and the lamp holders for the dashboard.

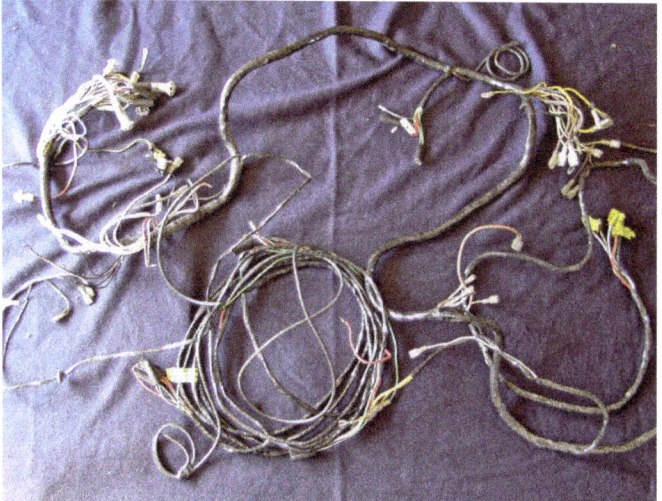

A complete replacement loom for my little Triumph Herald – it comes in only two parts, but makes spaghetti look neat!

in mind that it is designed to be removed, even if it doesn't appear so. Take your time and do not force the point; consult your manufacturer's literature if need be. A mirror can be useful in cases of restricted access.

Assess the job. Whilst de-trimming it should become apparent how the loom is laid out and how it must be handled in terms of logistics. As a rule, the last item out is the first to be refitted, but this depends on the sophistication of your vehicle.

Look for where the major bundles pass through the firewall.

Label everything. As I have stressed, it behoves us to label everything clearly and to tie groups of connections together. Work from the back of the car toward the

ENTHUSIAST'S RESTORATION MANUAL SERIES

firewall/bulkhead, starting in the boot area with the rear lamps and moving through the passenger compartment

In the engine compartment I would advise that you start with the lights. Keep the groups of wires together and label each connector individually before labelling them as a group. Next, disconnect the engine components. The HT set can be removed separately, as can other isolated sections such as the main earth and the starter lead. A few mechanically related leads such as the fuel sender unit, fuel pump, and reversing switch may have to be accessed from under the vehicle.

When dealing with a new loom, it will pay you to spend a bit of time laying it out across the vehicle and getting an idea of where the branches run before attempting to fit it. Where possible label the new connectors, as this will make fitment much easier.

SWITCHES
Manual switches

We are all familiar with the electrical switch. It is an everyday device used to open and close a huge variety of electrical circuits. And if asked to describe a typical switch, how many of us would resort to the word 'click'?

The click of a switch is actually an integral part of its function,

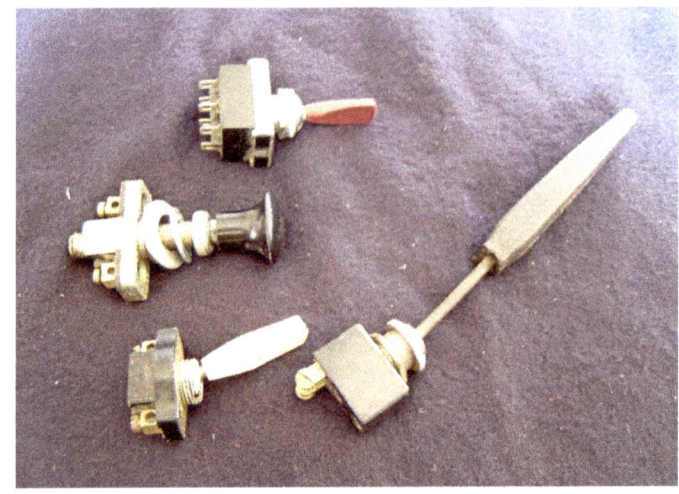

A selection of old switches show different connections.

Lovely old pull switch in the 'off' position ...

... and 'on'.

Mini light switch.

Variable resistor twist switch.

WIRES, FUSES & SWITCHES

for when connecting and more importantly when disconnecting the flow of electricity it is essential that no spark be present; sparking could pose a fire hazard and would also shorten the life of the switch contacts.

To this end it is normal for most switches to feature a spring, weight or even a magnet attached to one or both contacts.

Motor vehicle switches come in many shapes, sizes, and styles. Earlier items tend to feature screw terminals for wire attachment while those from the sixties onward are more likely to use spades (lucar) or push fit plugs. The very earliest switches might have been made of wood, porcelain, bakelite with mica, or other strange and wonderful insulators. Later items will more likely be made of moulded plastic.

Copper and brass have always been favoured as conductors and contacts as these materials give long trouble free service. You will also find steel contacts, and all are prone to corrosion if not kept clean and dry. Also, lack of use will tend to accelerate deterioration.

Your car's switch gear was designed to last the life of the vehicle, and since most of our classics have outlived their peers by several decades, failure is not unlikely.

The majority of automotive switches are not designed to be opened, but that does not always mean that repair is not possible. It often pays to carefully prise the unit apart, but only as a last resort.

My weapon of first choice would be a squirt from a can of 'Electrolube' or similar switch cleaner. This is available from any good electrical factors, and is essentially a fine solvent which will break up any oily deposit and remove any gum or dust.

When testing for continuity with a live tester, check either side of the unit before disconnecting the wires, then check the feed itself.

Rotary variable switches

Rotary switches such as volume or light dimmer switches are more correctly variabe resistors or 'potentiometers' – which is to say the dial is used to move one contact across a resistor, and depending on how much of that resistor is in circuit the current will be more of less attenuated.

Traditionally the resistor would take the form of a fine coil, Vehicles from the seventies will tend to feature carbon track switches (which we are all familiar with from nasty seventies hi-fis). These things pop and crack due to contamination!

Other switch gear

Many of the sensors and sender units

Gearbox switch. This can be used in conjunction with a gear linkage to ensure that the reverse light will only work in reverse.

fitted around our engines are, of course, switches. The oil pressure light is a sprung contact mounted behind a diapragm.

Heat sensors are often bimetallic switches which deform to move a contact either into or out of circuit. Other heat sensitive units rely on the change in resistance caused by a rise in temperature

The sender unit in your petrol tank is obviously very similar to the potentiometer described earlier.

AUTO ELECTRICAL CABLES AND THEIR APPLICATIONS (12V)

Contemporary guidebooks' recommended wiring

14 strand 0.010in copper cable for low current applications such as sidelights and indicators.
28 strand 0.012in copper cable for medium current applications such as headlamps and the heater fan. This also would be the choice when fitting foglamps, etc.
44 strand 0.012in copper cable for heavy-duty applications such as between the generator control box and battery, but not between the battery and starter motor.
Cable for use in the starter system is simply referred to as 'starter cable'. Bear in mind that it may have to handle 350A.
The earth strap is sold as such, and is not usually insulated.

Modern metric cable specifications

9 strand 0.3 mm copper cable 5.75A for low current applications such as sidelights and indicators.
14 strand 0.25mm copper cable 6A for radio and clock
14 strand 0.3 copper cable 8.75A for ignition LT.
28 strand 0.3 copper cable 17.5A for headlamps and heated rear screen.
44 strand 0.3 copper cable 27.5 for above dependent on spec.
65 strand 0.3 copper cable 35A for main applications such as generator and control box or battery. Dependent of output of generator.
84 strand 0.3 copper cable 45A also for above dependant on spec.
97 strand 0.3 copper cable 50A for alternator charging system – cable must match output of unit.
120 strand 0.3 copper cable 60A for alternator dependant on spec.
37 strand 0.9 copper cable 350A to 61 strand 0.9 700A is used for the starting system and must be able to handle maximum starting demand.

British Standard (BS) wiring colour codes 1986

Full colour codes for any vehicle can be found in the original workshop manual.
Black – earth.
Brown – main feed.
Blue/white – headlamp main beam.
Blue/red – headlamp dip beam.
Blue – headlamp switch to dip switch.
Blue/yellow – rear fog lamp.
Green – ignition controlled fused supply.
Green/red – side indicators left.
Green/white – side indicators right.
Light green – instruments.
Green/brown – reverse light.
Green/purple – rear brake lights.
Orange – windscreen wiper fused circuit.
Purple – constant live feed (un-fused).
Pink/white – ballast resistor (coil).
Red – sidelight main feed.
Red/black – sidelight left hand and number plate lamp.
Red/orange -sidelight right hand.
Slate – electric window lifters.
White – coil to ballast resistor.
White/black – igniton coil negative.

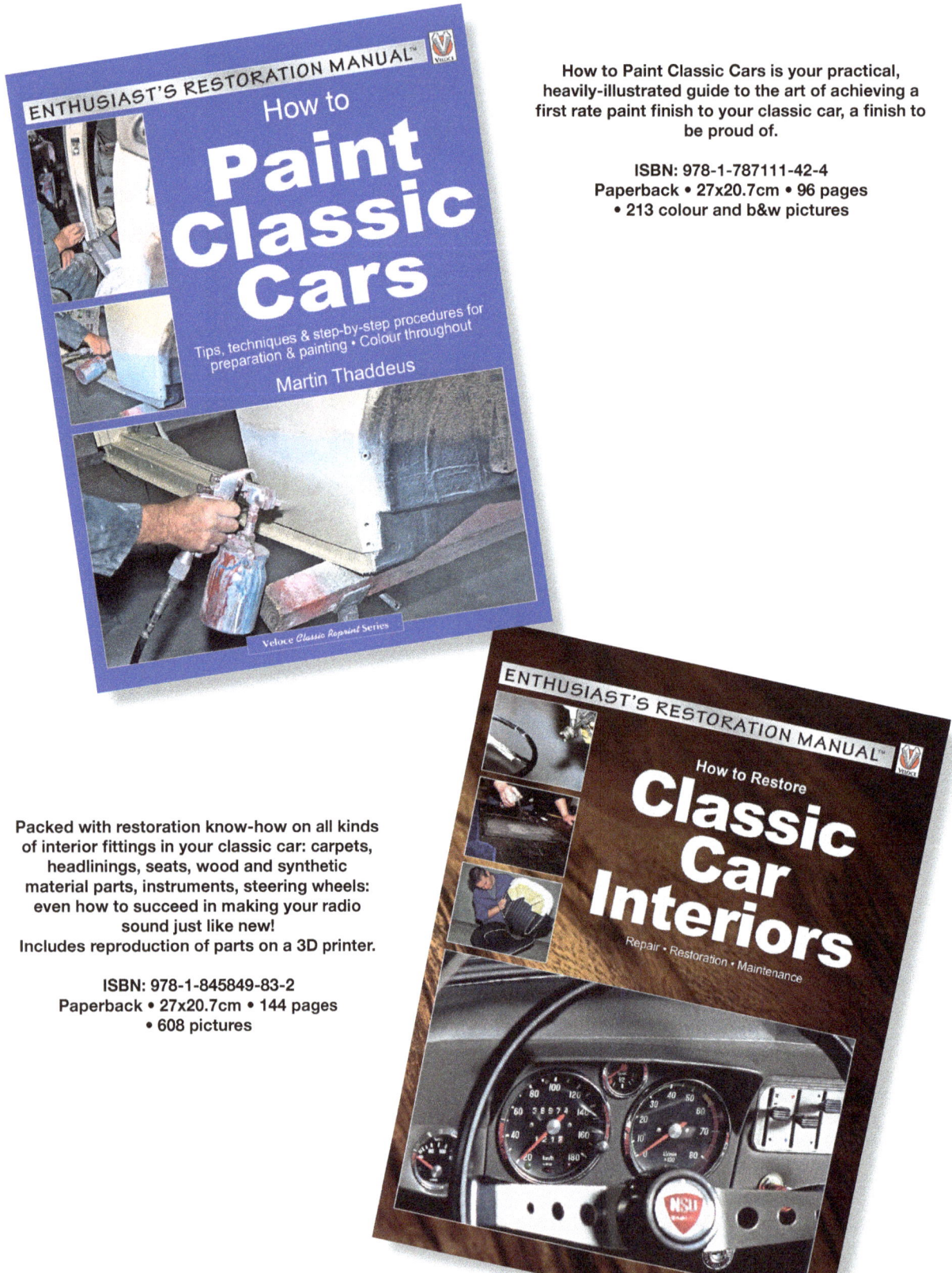

How to Paint Classic Cars is your practical, heavily-illustrated guide to the art of achieving a first rate paint finish to your classic car, a finish to be proud of.

ISBN: 978-1-787111-42-4
Paperback • 27x20.7cm • 96 pages
• 213 colour and b&w pictures

Packed with restoration know-how on all kinds of interior fittings in your classic car: carpets, headlinings, seats, wood and synthetic material parts, instruments, steering wheels: even how to succeed in making your radio sound just like new!
Includes reproduction of parts on a 3D printer.

ISBN: 978-1-845849-83-2
Paperback • 27x20.7cm • 144 pages
• 608 pictures

For more information and price details, visit our website at www.veloce.co.uk • email: info@veloce.co.uk
• Tel: +44(0)1305 260068

Completed at home by an enthusiastic DIY mechanic who has great experience rebuilding bikes, this book covers the complete restoration of a Triumph Trident T150V and a Triumph T160. Each and every aspect of the dismantling, refurbishment and reassembly of these classic bikes is covered in great detail, accompanied by a host of clear colour photos.

ISBN: 978-1-845848-82-8
Paperback • 27x20.7cm • 232 pages
• 704 colour pictures

A complete guide to the restoration of your VW Bus, with full coverage of body and chassis repairs, suspension, steering and brakes, plus trim and paint. It also covers the tools, equipment and workshop techniques needed to make your Bus look like new once more.

ISBN: 978-1-845840-93-8
Paperback • 27x20.7cm • 272 pages
• 1110 colour and b&w pictures

For more information and price details, visit our website at www.veloce.co.uk • email: info@veloce.co.uk
• Tel: +44(0)1305 260068

The definitive guide to restoring the Citroën 2CV and its close relatives the Dyane, Van, Ami 6 & Mehari. Aimed at the owner, here is a step-by-step, hands-on guide to every aspect of restoration including body, trim and mechanical components. Over 1400 colour photos illustrate every stage of the process.

ISBN: 978-1-903706-44-2
Paperback • 27x20.7cm • 272 pages
• 600+ pictures

Available again after a long absence! This book, which covers all Triumph TR2, 3, 3A, 4 & 4A models, explains the characteristics of the different models, what to look out for when purchasing and how to restore a TR cost effectively.

ISBN: 978-1-845849-47-4
Paperback • 27x20.7cm • 208 pages
• 500 pictures

For more information and price details, visit our website at www.veloce.co.uk • email: info@veloce.co.uk
• Tel: +44(0)1305 260068

Available again!
Written by an enthusiast the How to Restore Volkswagen Beetle Enthusiasts Restoration Manual is the only up-to-date book dealing with a complete Beetle restoration – from basic skills required, to dealing with professional restorers. The perfect book, whether you have no technical knowledge, or are an old hand at restoring!

ISBN: 978-1-845849-46-7
Paperback • 27x20.7cm • 224 pages
• c.700 colour pictures

The step-by-step guide to planning and restoring your car in the most cost-effective way. Includes body, trim and mechanical restoration, left- to right-hand drive conversion, clubs, specialists and suppliers, welding and restoration techniques, and advice on what work to sub-contract.

ISBN: 978-1-903706-46-6
Paperback • 27x20.7cm • 192 pages
• 450+ colour pictures

For more information and price details, visit our website at www.veloce.co.uk • email: info@veloce.co.uk
• Tel: +44(0)1305 260068

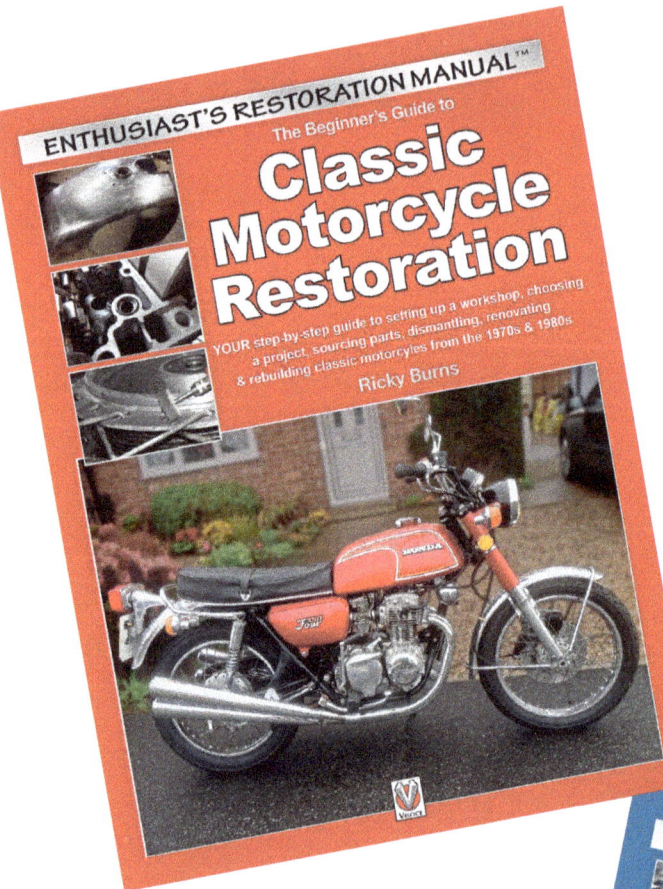

Seasoned motorcycle restorer Ricky Burns goes through each of the stages of a real-life restoration. Aimed at the total beginner but suitable for enthusiasts of all abilities, the reader is taken through each step in detail, and taught the techniques, tricks and tips used by experts. From choosing a project, setting up a workshop, and preparing a bike, to sourcing parts, dismantling, restoring and renovating, this book is the perfect guide for the classic motorcycle restorer.

ISBN: 978-1-845846-44-2
Paperback • 27x20.7cm • 144 pages
• 594 pictures

How to Restore Classic Off-road Motorcycles provides the classic off-road enthusiast with a step-by-step guide through a full restoration. Whether a post 1950 machine, or a more modern 80s twin shock, everything is covered in detail, from initial dismantling and parts sourcing to being ready to compete, including set-up and maintenance.

ISBN: 978-1-845849-50-4
Paperback • 27x20.7cm • 160 pages
• 488 colour pictures

For more information and price details, visit our website at www.veloce.co.uk • email: info@veloce.co.uk
• Tel: +44(0)1305 260068

Index

AC alternating current 16, 44
Accessory 14, 25, 30, 72
Alternator 8, 10, 26, 44-47
Ammeter 23, 78
Amp/ampere 23
Ancillary 30, 70
Atom 15
Auxiliary 30, 72

Ballast resistor 55
Battery 8, 11, 15, 17, 25, 31-37, 53
   charger 34
Battery charging 34
Booster cables/jump leads 34
Brushes motor/generator 38, 40, 47, 53
Bullet connector 81

Capacitor/condenser 54-62
Centrifugal advance 29, 59
Charge light 8
Charging – battery 34
Charging system 14, 25
Circuit diagram 18, 19
Circuit – series parallel 18
Circuit theory 17, 18
Coil-ignition 28, 54-62
Commutator 39, 40, 47, 54-62
Conductor 15
Connector – spade, Lucar, bullet, etc 16, 81-89
Contact breaker 28, 54-62
Control box voltage regulator 42-43

DC direct current 16, 38
Distributor 28, 55
Drive belt 40
Dwell 56
Dynamo 26, 38-43

Earth (positive and negative) 12, 16, 18
   Earth point 8, 16
Electrical theory 15
Electro magnet 20
Electrolyte 30
Electrons/electron flow 15, 17

Fan belt 40, 46
Flasher unit 69, 71
Fuse 62, 74, 81-89
Fuse board 82

Generator AC/DC 25, 38

Harness/loom 26
Heater fan 73
Horn 20, 72
HT high tension 28, 54-62
Hydrometer 37

Ignition system 10, 11, 14, 25, 28, 54-62
   Insulator 16

Joints – soldering 83
Jump leads, jump start 34, 35, 62

King lead 54

Leads – ignition 28, 54-62
Lighting 63-71
Live-tester 9, 11, 24, 25
Loom – wiring 29, 81-89
Loom swap 86
LT (low tension) 28, 54-62

Magnetism 20
Molecule 15
Motive force 17
Motor – starter 21
Multi-meter 7-9, 24, 52-54

Oil pressure gauge 78

Petrol gauge 78
Points – contact breaker 54-62
Polarity 16
Polarity change 46
Potentiometer 88

Radio 74
Relay 21

95

ENTHUSIAST'S RESTORATION MANUAL SERIES

Resistance – electrical 17, 23
Rotor arm 28, 55

Safety 10
Sealed beam headlamp unit 63, 64
Soldering a joint 83, 84
Sparkplugs 28, 47, 54-62
Speedometer 77
Starter motor 10, 27, 47, 50-52
Starter pinion 27, 47, 51, 52
Starter solenoid 21, 27, 47, 50, 51

Starter system 14, 25-27, 47
Stroboscope – timing light 9, 29, 60, 61
Surge protector 26, 62
Switches 63, 71, 88, 89

Tacho – rev counter 77
Temp gauge 78
Timing advance 29, 59
Timing – ignition static/dynamic 59, 60
Timing light – strobe 29

Vacuum advance 29
Variable resistor 88, 89
Volt/voltage 15, 17, 23, 37
Volt-meter 23, 36
Voltage regulator – control box 42, 44

Warning light – generator 8
Wires/wiring 26, 81
Wiring codes 89
Wiring diagram 19

www.velocebooks.com/www/veloce.co.uk
All books in print • New books Special offers Gift Vouchers

www.ingramcontent.com/pod-product-compliance
Lightning Source LLC
Chambersburg PA
CBHW040931240426
43672CB00023B/3000